SINGING AND SURVIVAL

SINGING AND
SURVIVAL

The Music of Easter Island

DAN BENDRUPS

OXFORD
UNIVERSITY PRESS

OXFORD
UNIVERSITY PRESS

Oxford University Press is a department of the University of Oxford. It furthers
the University's objective of excellence in research, scholarship, and education
by publishing worldwide. Oxford is a registered trade mark of Oxford University
Press in the UK and certain other countries.

Published in the United States of America by Oxford University Press
198 Madison Avenue, New York, NY 10016, United States of America.

CIP data is on file at the Library of Congress
ISBN 978–0–19–029704–6 (pbk.)
ISBN 978–0–19–029703–9 (hbk.)

9 8 7 6 5 4 3 2 1

Paperback printed by WebCom, Inc., Canada
Hardback printed by Bridgeport National Bindery, Inc., United States of America

CONTENTS

LIST OF FIGURES

PREFACE AND ACKNOWLEDGMENTS

Rapa Nui has its own night noises. There is always music, just a throb of it in the distance. There are voices and laughter rising above the pounding surf.

—CARLOTTA HACKER, *of the 1968 Canadian Medical Expedition to Easter Island (1968: 181)*

My first encounter with the music of Easter Island (or Rapa Nui) happened half a world away, in a Chilean migrant community festival in outer suburban Melbourne, Australia. In the late 1960s, a change in immigration policy enabled the first wave of migration of Chilean workers to Australia. They were soon followed by thousands of political refugees fleeing the Pinochet dictatorship (1973–1991). These groups mainly settled in Sydney and Melbourne, where they often converged with other recently arrived Latin American migrants but also maintained independent community events.

Some Chilean migrants were prominent in Melbourne's live music scene, especially in Latin dance bands, which experienced a surge in popularity from the Gypsy Kings–inspired "world music" boom of the late 1980s and early 1990s. As a trombonist trying to find my feet in the freelance gig economy, I found that the horn sections of these bands provided a ready source of income. I was also fortunate to have some contacts in the community, having grown up and gone to school in one of the areas where Chilean refugees and their children had settled. Overall, I spent almost a decade in and out of Latin bands in Melbourne, hanging out with Latin American musicians and later researching their contribution to Australian popular music (see Bendrups 2011b; Garrido and Bendrups 2013).

Many of these musicians also performed for community celebrations, such as Chilean Independence Day, where pan-Latin dance bands gave way to more nationalistic, folkloric performances. It was in this context that I first heard about Rapanui music. I soon discovered that the Chilean folk repertoire included a handful of songs that contained words from another language, performed with moves and guitar accompaniments that seemed more Hawaiian than Chilean. I thought little of it immediately, but over the years that followed, I became more curious about this cultural peculiarity. A respected musician in the Chilean-Australian migrant community once told me that the songs were from Rapa Nui, that the island was part of Chile, and that most Chileans learned a Rapanui song or two while at primary school, alongside other indigenous and folk songs. They were unlikely to be aware of the meanings of the songs, he said, or whether they had any special significance. But to leave them out, to not perform them, would be like failing to acknowledge an important part of Chile.

It intrigued me that this linguistically, culturally distinct music could be so stridently defended as central to Chilean culture and identity. From the little I had read, my understanding was that Rapanui culture had disappeared long ago, with only the iconic stone heads remaining to indicate the former presence of a unique civilization. But if this were true, how was it that these Chilean-Australian musicians possessed these songs, which sounded so different from every other kind of Chilean music I knew about?

In 2001, with the support of Philip Hayward and his research concerning small island music cultures across the Pacific, these questions became the basis for a doctoral research project. I began preparing myself for a lengthy period of ethnographic fieldwork on Rapa Nui, imagining that I would be working with a community much like the other Chilean communities I knew, but strangely transplanted to an exotic and isolated Pacific island.

Many of the available scholarly sources for traditional Rapanui music seemed to suggest that it had disappeared, or changed beyond recognition. For example, ethnographer Ramón Campbell, on returning to Rapa Nui in 1968, a few years after his initial research, encountered "purely Polynesian music, but very shambolic, with a mixture of different songs, texts, rhythms and dance. It was a potpourri completely lacking in ethnological and musical value" (Campbell 1971: 576). Similarly, folklorist Margot Loyola, who first visited Rapa Nui in 1961, returned there in 1975 and declared that "All had changed. Only the *moai* remained unaltered, staring into time infinite, but an evil wind blew against their faces and dark clouds obscured any rainbow" (Loyola 1988: 54). Based on these commentaries, I expected that my research would find remnants of an indigenous music culture that were somehow embedded in the musical lives of a community who now took their cultural cues from mainland, mainstream Chile.

I could not have been more wrong about this. The first inkling of my error was apparent en route to the island. While awaiting the midnight flight connection from Tahiti to Rapa Nui, I happened upon a group of Polynesian men who were conversing with each other in some sort of Spanish, mixed with what sounded like Tahitian. I approached the man in the queue ahead of me and attempted to strike up a conversation. His name was Uti Hereveri, a Rapanui fisherman who was heading home after a short visit to Tahiti.

Uti smiled at my fumbling attempts at small talk in the airport queue and asked why I was traveling to his island. I explained my research topic, which he absorbed with detached amusement and then quickly inquired about where I was planning to stay. This was something I hadn't really thought about yet. Uti insisted that I lodge with a friend of his, and then the boarding gate opened and I didn't see him again until we landed.

Arriving on Rapa Nui is exhilarating to the senses. Exiting the sterile, cool environs of the airplane, visitors are bombarded with moist tropical air carrying the scent of the grasses that coat the landscape. Approaching the terminal, as with elsewhere in Polynesia, visitors are welcomed with a musical performance of guitars and lilting melodies by musicians who probably have other things to do, but who are nonetheless committed to ensuring that the traveler's first impression is a positive one. Visitors alighting on the runway are observed from behind the airport perimeter fence by an assembly of islanders waiting for the return of their loved ones. Outside a cramped concrete bunker of a terminal, giant scoria sculptures offer artistic representations of the island's archaeological heritage. Uti found me in the chaos of the terminal and ushered me past security toward the exit, into the back seat of a well-weathered Volkswagen Kombi van belonging to his friend, Ana Maria "Meke" Edmunds Paoa. Meke and her family took me in, not knowing then that our relationship would endure over months of fieldwork and years of friendship.

Taking to the street to walk off my jet lag, I quickly realized that the Rapanui cultural demise promoted so readily in the global imaginary was vastly overstated. The Hangaroa streetscape bore many hallmarks of Chile, but the people were unlike any of the Chileans I had known throughout my life. The general store sold processed food from Latin America, but this was supplemented with locally grown taro and sweet potato, and fish taken straight from the sea. I saw immense tuna that would take pride of place in a metropolitan fish market being casually carved and distributed to the hands of children waiting to take it home for family lunches. While shopkeepers willingly greeted customers in Spanish, the lilt of Rapanui language was alive on every street corner. The Rapanui had not disappeared at all.

It turned out that Uti was quite a musician, which perhaps explained his amusement at the naivety of my research topic. Furthermore, he was at that very moment heavily involved in rehearsals for the annual Tapati Rapa Nui festival, and he decided that it would be instructive to bring me along so that I could observe exactly how alive Rapanui music really was. Not yet understanding any Rapanui language, I was uncertain of what he said to explain my unannounced presence at these rehearsals, but I have no doubt that it involved good-natured barbs along the lines of "opening his eyes" and "teaching this young foreigner a lesson or two about culture." Relationships are everything on Rapa Nui, and you only get one chance at a first impression. I was lucky that my first fumbling attempt at engagement was with Uti, a man of outstanding generosity and patience. One day on Rapa Nui had given me enough perspective to now realize that my whole research premise was misguided and that I would need to rethink my approach. I abandoned the idea of the doctorate as a study of Latin American cultural influence in Polynesia, instead focusing on documenting the living, thriving indigenous music culture into which my new friend had thrown me.

Initially, I dedicated my research efforts to seeking out and learning Rapanui songs. This turned out to be a great way to meet people, as songs tended to be associated with specific individuals within particular families. To learn a song correctly, one should really go to the most authoritative custodian. Some elders were recognized as being particularly knowledgeable, or in possession of special song repertoires that they may choose to share or not share, depending on who was asking and under what circumstances. One elder, Luis Avaka "Kiko" Pate Paoa, or Papa Kiko as he was known, was repeatedly recommended to me by other musicians.

Papa Kiko had participated in almost every significant Rapanui musical event of the twentieth century (see Bendrups 2007a). He was the custodian of ancient knowledge passed down by his grandmother, Rengahopuhopu, who had been born before the arrival of missionaries and colonists on Rapa Nui (McCall and Bendrups 2008). He had taught many of the performers now leading the island's active live music scene and had informed the important research conducted by Margot Loyola and Ramón Campbell in the 1960s (around half of the songs in Campbell's seminal 1971 collection are attributed to Kiko Pate). His voice had appeared on dozens of commercial and archival recordings (all held overseas), and he remained active in leading the Catholic Church choir for most Sunday services.

Papa Kiko was a gracious host. He especially enjoyed serving morning or afternoon tea to visitors, producing *pan amasado* (small Chilean rolls) or occasionally *sopaipillas* (fried pastry medallions), butter, and jam with barely concealed delight. He loved candy (*mona mona*), soap, and stuffed toy animals, which adorned every surface in the small cement sheet house in which he lived.

All of Papa Kiko's social graces were on display the day we met in 2002. No conversation could happen until tea was served. When the cups had been cleared away he turned to me, asking the question I'd been hoping for: "So, you're a musician, and you want to know about Rapanui music?" This was followed quickly by: "Well, I don't talk about music anymore. It's all there, all done. I told Doctor Campbell everything in nineteen-sixty . . . five?

Six, I think? Lots of people ask me but I tell them the same thing. It's done, *koti* (finished)." Our conversation then turned to the weather, as we watched a small raincloud forming over the Maunga Terevaka volcano. Our meetings over the course of the next few weeks followed this pattern. Papa Kiko would express his disinterest in talking about music, and then we'd talk about something else, all the while enjoying cups of tea.

A long-term Chilean resident on Rapa Nui once told me that the secret to building good relationships is *permanencia* (permanence), by which he meant "hanging around." Rapa Nui is inundated with passing tourists who don't usually stay long and who are often more interested in the island's archeological heritage than the descendants of those who created it. Many of the mainland Chileans who move to Rapa Nui for work do so with the understanding that they are only temporary migrants, and many do not seek to build enduring social relationships. Rapa Nui is frequently awash with researchers working on projects that have little bearing on contemporary life. Meanwhile, visitors claiming to be anthropologists in the past have actually turned out to be journalists, film or music producers, or, according to local legend, CIA agents. I was just the most recent example to have arrived at Papa Kiko's door. I needed more *permanencia*.

After about a month of casual visits, which began to include wide-ranging philosophical discussions about the meaning of culture and the purpose of music, Papa Kiko decided to progress our relationship by suggesting that we sing something together. I can't remember what song it was, but in hindsight, it was probably a test of sorts. Would it be worth making the effort to teach me? Would I be a quick enough learner? Would our voices be compatible? I must have passed the test, as, shortly thereafter, Kiko declared that perhaps there were some songs missing from Campbell's collection, and perhaps some of the songs Campbell had transcribed needed to be updated. But it would take time to think it through.

I left the island with a commitment from Papa Kiko that, when I returned in 2003, we would examine his repertoire, recording songs that might not be available elsewhere, and new versions of ones that he deemed needed correction. In 2003, over the course of about six months, I visited Papa Kiko on an almost daily basis and we worked through his personal and familial repertoire. This involved a particular process. Kiko would sing a line, then ask me to repeat it, then add the next line, and so on. Only when we reached the end of the song would he look over my annotations, and only when I could accompany him convincingly would he record it. From time to time, some of Papa Kiko's family members and former students would join us for these sessions, sometimes carrying their own notepads to jot down lyrics they were unfamiliar with or songs they hadn't heard for some time. After all, it's not every day that an elder custodian attempts to remember all of the songs he or she has learned over a lifetime of singing.

Working in this way with Papa Kiko became my entry point to the rich stream of knowledge through which Rapanui music is sustained. These songs provided my first lessons in the Rapanui language. They were also a means for engaging with others, as many of them were performed widely in the public domain. These songs also became a way of understanding Rapa Nui history and chronicling Rapanui survival. Some of them were very ancient, and some of them were not, but they all had something important to say about the lived experience of Rapanui people, whether in the distant or recent past. They provided a thread of continuity in a history of cultural change and adaptation.

REPRESENTING RAPA NUI

The research for this book draws on myriad conversations, formal and informal, and months of observation and participation in Rapanui music over the course of a decade. As postulated by Pacific historian Greg Dening (1996), the writing is itself a kind of performance, something crafted:

> We present our narratives with some theatricality. Our narratives also present something. They are ostensibly about something past, about something that has happened. But they are also the medium of our present relationships. (34)

The presence of Papa Kiko looms large in this narrative, accompanied by other knowledgeable musicians, many now deceased, who generously shared a short part of their lives with me. Except where specifically referenced, the stories contained in this book reflect the combined knowledge of various individuals, who told them to me from different perspectives or in various fragments that I subsequently wove together and rehearsed back to them for confirmation. Where knowledge of traditional or ancient performance practices are concerned, I am indebted to elders including María Elena Hotus, Alberto Hotus, Juan "Kakapa" Haoa, Papiano Ika, Antonio Tepano Hito, Marcos Rapu, and Frontier, who were not only great teachers but also willing collaborators in the transmission of their ancestral knowledge. Where knowledge of contemporary music is concerned, I owe sincere thanks to Kio Teao, Keva Atan, Sofía Abarca, Lynn Rapu, Pascual Pakarati, Mito Manutomatoma, Pete Pate, and Tomas Tepano, among many others.

My capacity to make sense of Rapanui society and culture was enriched by the support of many crucial friends, especially the Edmunds family and the Rapu-Tuki clan of the *frontera* (frontier). My time in mainland Chile was made possible thanks to the generosity of the Gibert family, and I am grateful to the many Chilean academics, folklorists, and musicians who allowed me to test out ideas with them over the last two decades. Throughout all of this, I thank Dr. Kerryn Bagley for her unwavering love and support.

The research for this book took place in different institutional contexts and with various sources of financial support, including a Macquarie University RAACE Scholarship and Research Grant, a University of Otago Research Grant, a Griffith University New Researcher Grant, and a La Trobe University Social Research Assistance Grant. All of the concepts, events, and repertoire items discussed in this book were encapsulated in my doctoral thesis, *Continuity in Adaptation: A History of Rapanui Music* (Bendrups 2006a), and some of them have also been discussed, with different scholarly emphases, in prior publications (specifically Bendrups 2006b, 2007b, 2009a, 2010, 2011c).

TYPOGRAPHIC CONVENTIONS
AND STYLE

At the time of writing, a standardized orthography for Rapanui language is still emerging. As noted by Kieviet (2016: 18), various orthographical options exist for the representation of vowel length, glottal plosives, and the velar nasal phoneme in written Rapanui language. This book employs a simplified approach in which vowel lengths are not marked diacritically. Glottal plosives are indicated by an inverse "curled" apostrophe, and the velar nasal phoneme is rendered as "ng," throughout.

All Rapanui and Spanish words (except for proper nouns), as well as song, book, and album titles, are rendered in italics. Direct quotations from Spanish and French sources, as well as Rapanui and Spanish song lyrics, have been translated into English by the author. In keeping with current convention, Rapa Nui is used throughout to refer to the island, while the conjoined "Rapanui" refers to society, culture, language, and people. The term "precontact" replaces "prehistoric" in regard to aspects of Rapanui life that predate European contact (after Moulin 1996).

The personal names of Rapanui musicians in this book appear with their permission. Following Rapanui custom, individuals are usually referred to by nickname rather than by their full name, unless they have requested otherwise (the respected musician Sergio Teao Atan, for example, was known as "Kio Teao" or simply "Kio" in his community, and that convention is followed in this book). This practice connotes both respect and recognition, and is preferable to the use of surnames because it reflects familiarity.

This book does not contain any restricted knowledge or knowledge that is subject to any other known cultural protocols.

SINGING AND SURVIVAL

INTRODUCTION

Rapanui Music in Context

> Ancient music has disappeared, with the exception of
> two songs which, though not very old, seem to give a
> faint idea of the rhythm and character of the genuine
> native music.
>
> —ETHNOLOGIST ALFRED MÈTRAUX, *in his*
> Ethnology of Easter Island *(1940: 355)*

SWISS-ARGENTINE ETHNOLOGIST ALFRED MÈTRAUX
WROTE one of the most celebrated early accounts of Rapanui
culture, but there is palpable disappointment in his appraisal
of the traditional Rapanui music he encountered in the 1930s.
Along with the apparent disappearance of "ancient" music, the
two remnant songs he described seemed to have quite unre-
markable, mundane lyrics. One related a Rapanui experience
of contact with (supposedly) Chinese sailors some years prior,
considered noteworthy by Mètraux (1940) because "it was the
first time the natives had seen men with long hair and wrist
watches" (355). The other was a "short satirical song" composed
around 1890, which "tells of the marital disgrace of Aru-manu-
vie, a famous fisherman, whose wife had been stolen by a certain Rahi" (355). Mètraux transcribed and translated the texts
of these two songs in his seminal ethnology and then moved on
to other topics.

Mètraux's consideration of precisely what constituted "ancient" music was likely based on expectations about musical form, rather than considerations of musical function. The range of acculturated influences present in Rapanui music of the 1930s would indeed have made it difficult for an outsider to ascertain exactly which bits of it might reflect ancient practices. Mètraux didn't provide notated transcriptions, but it is unlikely that a formal analysis would have yielded further insight anyway.

However, from a Rapanui perspective, the first song, *I rari te reka hiva*, could be understood as fulfilling an ancient purpose. Traditionally, Rapanui songs served as vehicles for preserving events of importance in the historical record. The second song, *Rahi toke vi'e*, was an example of *'ei*, a song of ridicule—a traditional performance genre that Mètraux described in detail elsewhere in his writings (Mètraux 1957: 179). In terms of function, both of these songs were excellent examples of the continuity of precontact Rapanui musical heritage.

Unbeknownst to Mètraux, his expedition to Rapa Nui served as a catalyst for musical renewal. His research team traversed the island, attended by Rapanui assistants who would otherwise have been barred from visiting their ancestral lands at this time. The elders of this group took advantage of their evenings encamped together to share songs and stories with their younger counterparts. In his old age, respected elder Juan Haoa remembered how formative this experience had been for him as a young boy. The expedition gave his elders a context for knowledge sharing, an opportunity to keep their songs strong.

Hailing from the world's most remote site of human settlement and having endured a history of slave raids, introduced disease, Christian conversion, a despotic takeover, land dispossession, military governance, and neocolonialism, generations of Rapanui have adapted their cultural practices to changing circumstances while retaining threads of cultural continuity with which to weave a connection between their changing present and their ancient past. This is reflected in efforts toward language preservation; in the telling and retelling of ancient stories; in the preservation of traditional farming, fishing, and cooking methods; and in the continuity of a vibrant performance culture in which songs and singing are paramount.

This book aims to demonstrate music's important role in the sustainability of Rapanui cultural heritage. It seeks to convey to the reader an understanding of performance that extends beyond aesthetic considerations to an appreciation of what it means for a once-endangered culture to survive—and to thrive—and the contribution that music can make to this process. It is an argument for music not only as a cultural practice of intrinsic value but also as a means of cultural survival. In the pursuit of this argument, it reveals how the Rapanui have carefully nurtured ancestral knowledge passed down over generations, as well as embracing a world of trans-Pacific cultural flows, drawing inspiration from waves of contact with Latin America, with other Polynesian peoples, and with globalized elements of Western popular culture.

The need for such a discussion is great where Rapa Nui is concerned. This solitary island provides a rare example of an indigenous culture rebounding from population decline so dramatic as to be almost terminal. The survival of Rapanui culture, in any of its manifestations, is a tale worth telling. Meanwhile, there are few places in the world so thoroughly represented in global discourses of cultural collapse as Rapa Nui, and the propensity for Rapa Nui to be presented as a case study in anthropogenic destruction makes the telling of a redemptive story of cultural survival and sustainability all the more important. In the global imaginary, the Rapanui people are frequently consigned to the realm of disappeared "prehistoric" societies, written out of their own history. This study of continuity and adaptation in Rapanui music culture provides a counterpoint to this deficit discourse, instead presenting Rapanui music as evidence of continuity in cultural practice.

This introduction provides a contextual discussion that is necessary for understanding the sequence of chapters that follow. To begin with, it offers a social history of Rapa Nui that describes the various forces that have effected change in Rapanui society, extending from precontact times to the 1960s—the point at which the Rapanui people were recognized as Chilean citizens, and the point at which international engagement through tourism commenced in earnest. This history includes a short detour through the discourses of collapse and "ecocide" that permeate Rapanui scholarship. This is followed by a discussion of music and sustainability that provides a theoretical and disciplinary grounding for the study. Finally, this introduction provides an explanation of the structure of the book and the chapters that follow.

RAPANUI HISTORY IN CONTEXT

Rapa Nui is a small subtropical Pacific island located more than one thousand miles from the nearest habitable island (Pitcairn Island) and over two thousand miles from the nearest mainland (South America). The island's Polynesian settlers, who arrived around or before the thirteenth century AD (Stevenson et al. 2015), transported cultural practices consistent with those of wider Polynesia, including a funerary tradition of raising elaborate headstones for the deceased (Flenley and Bahn 2003: 103; McCall 1994). This practice was intensified on Rapa Nui over generations, resulting in the world heritage monuments for which the island is known today: ancient monoliths called *moai aringa ora* (or just *moai*), the "living faces" of the ancestors.

A conventional (though now contested) telling of precontact Rapanui history is that the intensification and expansion of *moai* building consumed the island's resources, possibly leading to conflict over dwindling food sources and the subsequent abandonment of *moai* building and worship (Flenley and Bahn 2003: 82; Bork and Mieth 2003; Flannery 1994: 257; van Tilburg 1994). Over time, sacred sites were destroyed or ruined, and settlments abandoned in favor of fortified cave dwellings that suggest occurances of inter-clan conflict. These changes were already in motion when Dutch explorer Jacob Rogeveen encountered the island on Easter Sunday of 1722, hence the name Easter Island. The name "Rapa Nui" (also rendered Rapanui, meaning the "large raft") is more recent, stemming from contact with other Polynesians in the late nineteenth century. Prior to this, the ancient Rapanui called their land Te Pito o te Henua, the "navel" or "center" of the earth.

Eighteenth-century visitors to Rapa Nui marveled at the island's stone giants. Captain Felipe González y Haedo, who claimed the island for Spain in 1770, observed *moai* still standing, while Captain James Cook, in 1774, described statues toppled in disarray. As Western influence in the Pacific expanded in the nineteenth and early twentieth centuries, Rapa Nui emerged as a subject of fascination in global popular culture. How could a (seemingly) Stone Age society of cave dwellers have produced stonework to rival the majesty of the pyramids of Giza, or Stonehenge on the Sailsbury Plain, on a solitary island so incredibly remote? Between the 1880s and the 1950s, major ethnographic and archaeological expeditions were dispatched to Rapa Nui from Europe and North America, as well as from mainland Chile, in search of answers.

Throughout the twentieth century, Western fascination with Rapa Nui has been reflected in books ranging from those that simply remarked on the apparent mystery presented by Easter Island (Macmillan-Brown 1926) to those that offered fanciful extraterrestrial explanations for the island's unique stone works (von Däniken 1968). Meanwhile, Thor Heyerdahl's

(1972) theory (now discredited) of a Latin American origin for the ancient Rapanui people offered a tantalizing alternative explanation of prehistoric global migrations. These ideas, whether science or science fiction, became embedded in Western popular culture, reflected in books, films, comics, cartoons, and video games from the 1960s to the present (see Conrich and Mückler 2016).

Recent research has produced greater insight into the questions of how the island of Rapa Nui came to be settled (Hunt and Lipo 2006). DNA analysis confirms a Polynesian origin for the Rapanui people (Fehren-Schmitz et al. 2014) but leaves open the possibility that their Polynesian ancestors may have also voyaged to and from the Americas. While studies have largely confirmed deforestation and its effects on food production as a challenge for precontact Rapanui society, preceding the demise of *moai* culture, the presumption that this decline was rapid and uncontrolled, or even attributable to human factors, has been questioned (Larsen and Simpson 2014). Nevertheless, the presumed role of the ancient Rapanui people in bringing about their own ecological "collapse" has powerful resonances for the contemporary world. Writers have seized upon this, pointing to ancient Rapa Nui as a cautionary tale about the perils of environmental destruction (most famously Diamond 2005, but also Flannery 1994 and Ponting 1991). While well intentioned, works such as these are largely based on second- or third-hand interpretations of Rapanui research and tend to essentialize a situation that is only partially understood. They largely ignore the proactive agricultural strategies developed by the Rapanui to respond to their changing environment (see, e.g., Stevenson et al. 2015), which tell a different story from the more sensational tropes of collapse and ecocide. They also have the unfortunate effect of reinforcing the myth that the Rapanui people brought about the end of their own civilization.

To the contrary, the Rapanui people survived, establishing a new social equilibrium. One outcome of this was the development of a ritual in which social authority was vested in the winner of an annual competition of strength and endurance, the *tangata manu*, or "bird man" competition. Each year, prospective *tangata manu* from different clans would appoint one or more *hopu* ("assistants," or perhaps "lieutenants") to undertake a perilous cliff descent and ocean swim to the offshore islet of Motu Nui, where they would await the arrival of the migrating *manutara* (sooty tern). The first *hopu* to find a *manutara* egg would be declared the victor, and his sponsor would be declared *tangata manu* and invested with special privileges (such as authority over food distribution). This ritual endured well into the nineteenth century.

As Benny Peiser (2005) elegantly explains, the most serious threat to the survival of the Rapanui people and their culture was not self-induced ecocide, but the impact of Western commercial and cultural expansion in the nineteenth-century Pacific. From the 1720s onward, the Rapanui negotiated sporadic instances of contact with foreigners, with a mix of positive and negative effects. In 1805, a North American sealing expedition stopped at Rapa Nui and abducted a number of islanders with the intention of relocating them as a captive workforce on the uninhabited island of Más Afuera (Alejandro Selkirk Island) in the Juan Fernández archipelago (Wilhelm 1935: 12). This early instance of slaving was a precursor to a more extensive "blackbirding" enterprise for plantation labor and guano mining in Peru (see Maude 1981). Between 1862 and 1863, Rapa Nui was used as a staging ground for slave taking raids in Eastern Polynesia, with dire consequences for the local population. Of the 1,704 Polynesians transported to Peru, 1,400 are believed to have been from Rapa Nui (Fischer 2001: 279). Three hundred and eighteen Rapanui islanders were eventually repatriated to the protection of the Catholic diocese in Papeete, but eighty-five died from smallpox during the voyage, and only fifteen survived to reach Rapa Nui, where the exotic diseases they were carrying caused the deaths of an estimated 1,000 more islanders (Englert 1964: 14; 1995: 123; Fischer 2001: 54). This period was highly destructive to Rapanui society, depriving the community of leaders and culture bearers, and setting the scene for further disruption in the ensuing decades.

The establishment of a Sacred Heart mission on Rapa Nui in 1864 coincided with the society's efforts to recover from the sharp population decline of the previous years, and the Catholic Church became pivotal to the renewal of Rapanui culture. The mission's supply chain created opportunities for new visitors to engage with Rapa Nui. It was in this context that French merchant sailor Jean Baptiste Onézime Dutrou-Bornier encountered Rapa Nui, noted the unprotected and dwindling population, and took the opportunity to seize control over much of the island for himself (Englert 1964: 51). The missionaries resisted Dutrou-Bornier but were ultimately bested, and they fled Rapa Nui in 1871 together with around 400 followers, leaving only 175 people behind. In 1876, after five years of exploitative rule, Dutrou-Bornier was beaten to death by two of his exasperated lieutenants. When pioneering travel writer Auguste Pinart visited the island the following year, he encountered a reported population of just 110 people. It is from this population base that the present-day Rapanui society has been rebuilt.

In 1888, a Chilean delegation arrived to offer protection to the Rapanui in return for the annexation of their island, and they agreed, establishing the Rapanui connection to South America that endures to the present day. However, after two failed attempts to establish a colony, the management of the island, and of the Rapanui people themselves, was ceded to one private pastoral company, and then another, before coming under direct administration by the Chilean navy (see Porteous 1981). Only in the 1950s did it become possible for Rapanui people to travel from their island, and only in 1966 were they recognized as Chilean citizens. While some Rapanui consider themselves proudly Chilean, the exploitation and dispossession the Rapanui experienced over decades of neglect by Chile are reflected in the community's complex and sometimes hostile relationship with the Chilean state (see McCall 1975) and permeate through ongoing discussions of independence and self-determination.

MUSIC AND SUSTAINABILITY

As this history illustrates, the Rapanui people (and their culture) have faced particular threats since the intensification of European activity in the Pacific in the mid-nineteenth century. And yet, despite the catastrophic events of the 1860s and 1870s, they managed to survive, retaining a suite of unique performance practices in the process. The *moai* carved by their ancestors also survived, becoming icons of world heritage and subject to various restoration projects from the 1950s onward. This laid the groundwork for an emergent tourism industry that now predominates in all aspects of Rapanui life and that, notwithstanding some inconsistencies in distribution and engagement, provides income to support a quality of life unimaginable only a generation ago. Because of this, the discourses of heritage and culture loom large in contemporary Rapanui society.

Where the *moai* and other archeological treasures are concerned, protocols informed by the cultural heritage principles of preservation, conservation, and sustainability have emerged and strengthened over recent decades. Many archeological sites that were once open to grazing by horses or trampling by tourists have now been fenced off and controlled, and any tourist now touching or climbing on a *moai* is met with condemnation and the possibility of police detention. The Rapanui may have lost their former religious connections to the living faces of their ancestors, but this has been replaced by a new kind of reverence steeped in respect for the *moai* as symbols of an ancient and unique cultural heritage. This sensibility has also infused contemporary Rapanui attitudes toward aspects of their intangible cultural heritage, including music.

Rapanui music is well placed for inclusion in the discourse of sustainability that has emerged in twenty-first-century ethnomusicology and anthropology. Linked to broader discussions around applied research (Pettan and Titon 2015) and the preservation of intangible cultural heritage on the one hand, and to discussions of acoustic ecology and musical "ecosystems" on the other (see Schippers and Bendrups 2015; Bendrups and Barney 2013), the discourse of sustainability is one of the more significant features of early twenty-first-century ethnomusicology.

This collective interest in sustainability (as reflected in works such as Grant and Schippers 2016 and Grant 2014) reflects changes felt more widely in contemporary cultural heritage discourses. Twenty-first-century advances in global mobility and connectivity have engendered a broader awareness of the issues and challenges facing global cultural diversity, leading to new frameworks for cultural preservation, sustainability, and renewal, designed and promoted at a global level (UNESCO 2003, 2005; United Nations 2007). Heritage has an important place in these discussions, understood not just in terms of protecting the past, but in a more complex context of ongoing social engagement between people and places, and the ongoing construction of meaning derived from this interaction (Auclair and Fairclough 2015: 3–9). As with Palazzo and Pugliano's (2015) description of contemporary Roman citizens negotiating life within an archeological site, surrounded by heritage, so too are the Rapanui people constantly reminded of the material legacy of their ancestors. This constant reminder ultimately affects the collective identity of the community, as expressed through performance.

The discourse of sustainability has one particular benefit for ethnomusicology, as it provides a theoretical frame for moving beyond some of the dyadic constructs that have otherwise guided past ethnomusicological thought, including the ideas of "invented" tradition and "acculturation" (or for that matter "assimilation") of musical practices. All of these constructs assume a "before" and an "after," or an "authentic" and an "inauthentic." Music sustainability, meanwhile, asks not what is being sustained but why, and by whom, according to what priorities. Sometimes priorities are set by the state, but at other times, direct engagement in priority setting is a means for marginalized or minority groups to gain agency in the means of their own cultural representation.

This way of thinking has a long history in Pacific music research. For example, in 1981, Allan Thomas was already advocating for so-called "cheap and tawdry borrowed tunes" from popular Western music to be appreciated as vectors for indigenous cultural heritage and identity (Thomas 1981). Some years later, Jane Moulin (1996) made a rousing call for contemporary Pacific cultures to be valued for their sheer survival in the face of centuries of European imperial and colonial interference. These sentiments were shared more broadly in the Pacific cultural studies of the 1990s, as reflected in the writings of Margaret Jolly and others (Jolly 1992; Jolly and Thomas 1992).

PERSPECTIVES ON RAPANUI MUSIC

With this music sustainability ethos in mind, this book presents various overlapping perspectives on Rapanui music that each articulate a different way of understanding change and continuity in Rapanui performance culture and social life. Each of the chapters follows an internal chronological order, but they all overlap with each other in the broader passage of time. The first chapter, "Singing and Survival," aims to provide a thorough description of the known elements of Rapanui music as passed down from precontact times. This chapter draws on explorers' descriptions and early ethnographic accounts, as well as knowledge collected through participant observation fieldwork, to construct a comprehensive picture of ancient, "ancestral," or traditional music.

The second chapter, "Religion and Renewal," considers Rapanui musical development in terms of the cultural influence of the Catholic Church. Sacred Heart missionaries arrived on Rapa Nui in the 1860s and subsequently played a considerable role in the community's cultural renewal, including interactions with the outside world. The Church has since had a central role in Rapanui social and musical life, which this chapter seeks to convey.

The third chapter, "Chilean Culture," offers a discussion of Chile's interactions with Rapa Nui before, during, and after the island's annexation. This chapter considers not only the direct impact of Chilean cultural imports on Rapanui music but also the ways in which Chile acted as a conduit to influences from a broader pan-American cultural context. It is through Chile, for example, that the Rapanui became acquainted with tango, leading to the creation of a unique local variant of this music and dance genre.

The fourth chapter, "Polynesian Pathways," considers interactions between Rapanui and other Polynesians, and the impact of these interactions on Rapanui music. The relationship to Polynesia, especially Tahiti and, more recently, New Zealand and Hawaii, is central to Rapanui constructions of identity and provides a counterpoint to prevailing cultural influence from Chile. This has been manifested in musical choices, including the adoption and adaptation of particular elements of pan-Pacific performance practice.

The final chapter, "Commercial Connections," considers Rapanui music in relation to global commercial influences, especially those emanating from the United States. This chapter reveals how Rapanui performers since the 1960s have made sense of global cultural influences, and how these have in turn been represented on the island itself. It also considers the capacity for Rapanui performers to extend beyond the confines of Chilean folklore performance contexts and into mainstream global popular culture, providing key examples of groups and individuals who have achieved some level of national or international popularity.

1

SINGING AND SURVIVAL

> The music of the Tahitians is happy and easy; that of
> Easter Island is strangely sad, composed of short phrases
> [with] inaudible endings. The men sing with a sorrowful
> voice, which has nothing natural about it. . . . I wanted to
> write down some of their airs but it is impossible, our
> notation is insufficient.
>
> — PIERRE LOTI, *describing performances observed on a visit to*
> *Rapa Nui in 1872, in his 1899 travelogue* Reflets sur la Sombre Route
> *(1988 [1899]: 38)*

FRENCH TRAVEL WRITER, POET, AND illustrator Pierre Loti
arrived on Rapa Nui in 1872, just as the community was trying
to make sense of a decade of tumultuous change. Contact with
the outside world had decimated Rapanui society in the 1860s,
with slave taking and introduced disease claiming up to four-
fifths of the population. Now, for the first time, outsiders had a
hand in Rapanui daily life. Missionaries and Christian worship
had displaced ancient ritual and religious practices, and the
marooned French-Tahitian ship's captain Jean Baptiste Dutrou-
Bornier had declared himself "king" of Rapa Nui.

The performances described by Loti were remnants of cultural practices that scarcely a decade before had served the social
and ceremonial needs of a community of perhaps five thousand
people, now reduced to little more than a hundred. And yet
these performances endured. At a time of almost unimaginable
social crisis, and under the increasing influence of new, foreign

cultural forces, the Rapanui were persevering with a musical culture both distinguishable from that of other Polynesians and, by Loti's account, completely alien to European ears.

It is unlikely that the performers of the 1870s were in possession of the full social and ritual repertoires of their ancestors, as too many had perished in the preceding decade. However, performances were still a vehicle through which the stories of the past could be told, and songs served a meaningful range of functions in people's interactions with each other. These roles for music in social interaction were kept strong, providing the basis for a cultural revival that endured throughout the twentieth century. The purpose of this chapter is to present an account of the musical practices that were preserved in the 1870s and which have come to be considered the core of Rapanui "traditional" music. This account is informed by the observations of early explorers, renditions of oral history captured in nineteenth- and twentieth-century ethnographies, and details drawn from my own ethnographic fieldwork on Rapa Nui in the early 2000s.

TRADITIONAL PERFORMANCE CONTEXTS

The role of music and dance in Rapanui social relations was reflected in the reports of early European explorers. According to Fischer (2005), the first islander to board Dutch explorer Jacob Rogeveen's mast ship in 1722 promptly chanted recitations, possibly aimed at lifting *tapu* (spiritual prohibition) associated with the unnaturally pale visitors, and proceeded to offer a song of welcome. A few days later, Rogeveen's approach to Hanga o Honu (Turtle Bay) was greeted by hosts "hopping and dancing for joy" (Fischer 2005: 50), which is probably an early observation of the performance genre now known as *hoko*.

These danced and chanted greetings featured in Rapanui-European interactions again a century later, as depicted in the 1838 drawing of a *danse à cloche-pied* (hopping dance) by Louis Joules Masselot (Figure 1.1). The islanders in this depiction were seemingly unperturbed by European contact: they approached and boarded Masselot's ship, the *Venus*, and once on board, they proceeded to dance, with one performer even wearing a European sailor's hat.

Another description of Rapanui music comes from the journal of English explorer F. W. Beechey, whose four-year expedition through the Pacific stopped at Rapa Nui in 1826. Beechey (1831) described a reception in which

Danse à cloche-pied des Indigènes de l'île de Pâques.

FIGURE 1.1. *Danse à cloche-pied des indigenes de l'ile de Paques.* The "hopping dance" sketched by Louis Joules Masselot, c.1838, published in the "Picturesque Atlas" of the Voyage of the *Venus* (Paris: Gide, 1841). Reproduced with permission, Alexander Turnbull Library, Wellington, New Zealand.

a very young girl [was] recommended to the attention of one of the officers, who, in compassion, allowed her a seat in his boat. . . . [She] then commenced a song not altogether inharmonious. . . . As our party passed, the assemblage of females on the rock commenced a song, similar to that chanted by the lady in the boat; and accompanied it by extending their arms over their heads, beating their breasts, and performing a variety of gestures, which showed that our visit was acceptable, at least to that part of the community. (45–46)

Along with the apparent role of music in fostering intercultural encounters, early ethnographic accounts suggest a vital role for performance in social cohesion, ritual, and celebration. In the 1860s, the first missionary dispatched to Rapa Nui, Eugène Eyraud, observed that "the celebrations are continuous; when they finish at one end of the island, they begin again at the other" (quoted in Campbell 1988: 55). This was echoed fifty years later by anthropologist Katherine Scoresby Routledge (1998: 233), who asserted that the Rapanui would make almost any excuse for a celebration.

According to ethnographic accounts, the precontact Rapanui used the ceremonial platforms, or *ahu*, found at each of the hamlets that surround their island, as the physical space and social context for rituals and celebration. Music, dance, and dramatized performances were designated to occur in the space *he mu'a o te ahu*—literally, "in front of the *ahu*" (Englert 1970: 178). Sometimes, rituals incorporated the *tahua* of the *ahu*—a raised earth section covered with smooth stones, which served as a burial site for clan leaders (Figure 1.2). On other occasions, a structure called a *kaunga*, a dancing ground consisting of "a narrow strip paved with pebbles, over 200 feet in length by 2 feet in width and not unlike the paved approach to some *ahu*" (Routledge 1998 [1919]: 234–35), was used as a performance space.

FIGURE 1.2. Restored *ahu*. A photograph of *ahu* Akivi showing staging ground in front of the raised platform and *moai*. This ahu is the subject of the song *Ahu Akivi*, described in detail in Chapter 4.

Historically, community-wide celebrations (collectively called *ngongoro*) were known to have existed. Examples preserved in Rapanui oral history include events such as *koro paina*, or just *paina* (a festival of thanksgiving for one's father), and *paina tuhi renga*, or "festival of presentation" (also called *hikinga kaunga* by Englert [1970: 178]). According to Routledge (1998 [1919]: 233), the *paina* celebration involved the construction of an effigy (also called a *paina*) made from woven rods and *mahute* paperbark cloth, and a crown made of *makohe* (Frigate Bird) wings. It is understood that the person responsible for commissioning the celebration would go inside the effigy and lead the ceremony from within, speaking through the figure's mouth.

In the 1930s, ethnologist Alfred Mètraux made similar observations, ascribing the term *koro* to both the feast and the house (*hare koro*) where it took place. He also noted the *paina*, another festival called *are auti,* and the *tangata manu,* or "bird man" competition (which had persisted through to the 1860s), as important festival occasions (Mètraux 1940: 343). To this list of celebrations, Mètraux added *puke,* a ceremony where seaweed-wielding adults sought to divine the longevity of children, and *kaunga,* a feast for young people, performed on paved platforms (350–51). Other events such as *koro hakaopo* song contests and *koro tuha moa* (also known as a *ngorongoro moa*) for the public distribution of chickens, a dietary staple, are also said to have occurred in front of the *ahu* (Englert 1995: 70, 236).

While all of these celebrations would have included some form of performance, only the *koro hakaopo* was considered to have been concerned primarily with music. While extant descriptions define *koro hakaopo* as pertaining to a song "possessed of good meaning" (see McLean 1999: 286), it may also be described as a song contest between competing ensembles. In contemporary Rapanui culture, the *koro hakaopo* has been preserved as a featured event in the annual Tapati Rapa Nui festival celebrations, lasting from nightfall through to the early hours of the morning.

Other festivals mapped important life cycle events and seasonal ceremonies. According to the oral record, prior to the arrival of missionaries, groups of specially selected Rapanui children (called *neru*) were isolated from society for a time in secluded caves on the Poike peninsula, where their activities likely included learning performances related to history and ritual (Arredondo 2004: 73–74). This probably included songs, chants, and their associated visual and gestural accompaniments, which the *neru* would perform in ceremonial contexts. Similarly, some Rapanui believe that the cave called Ana Kai Tangata, near Hangaroa, was used seasonally as a site for secluded tuition, as the word *kai,* or "food," might also denote intellectual nourishment. This cave is considered to be of special ceremonial significance because of the detailed rock paintings that adorn its ceiling.

TRADITIONAL ENSEMBLE ORGANIZATION

There is no record of formal performance ensembles existing in precontact Rapanui culture. Rather, ensembles of performers, called *huru riu*, would be assembled on an as-needed basis, commissioned by a *motuha* (a patron) and organized by a *hatu* (ensemble leader). While performance does not appear to have been subject to many (if any) restrictions for adult performers, it is likely that the role of *hatu* was a specialized one within extended families, with certain *hatu* retaining this role for life.

According to available descriptions of formal performances, singers were sorted into sections by gender. Female singers (*pepere*, or *ihi*) and male singers (*pere*) were arranged in parallel lines (men standing behind, women kneeling in front) to either side of the *hatu*, all facing the same direction (Mètraux 1940: 357; Englert 1995: 231). Some seated performers could manage large stone percussion (with one stone placed on the ground and the other held between the hands), while others would have hands free for gesturing, with hand and arm movements symbolizing key elements of the song text, in a manner similar to Tahitian 'aparima.

The songs for these performances were either responsorial (where the *hatu* would begin a phrase, to be answered by the group) or strophic, with the *hatu* leading each verse and other singers gradually joining in. Songs usually consisted of short, predictable, repeated phrases that enabled participation and that allowed the *hatu* to extend or shorten a given song depending on the mood of the audience or the need of the occasion.

Traditionally, songs were written with a single melody line in mind, sung in unison or parallel octaves, possibly accompanied by a drone. However, the flexibility of entry and exit points in each verse, the difference in pitch between male and female voices, and the interplay between possible drone lines and a moving melody line provided scope for harmonic development in ensemble performances. Melodies with flat contours provided confident singers with opportunities to experiment with impromptu harmonies, departing from the melody line, and the descending melismatic phrase endings typical of a particularly ancient performance genre (called *riu tuai*) provided tonal reference points at the equivalent of the "dominant" and "tonic" scale degrees, setting up another context for incidental harmony to occur. The ancient Rapanui had no known system for ascertaining fixed pitches; rather, the tonal "center" of any song was determined by the vocal range deemed comfortable to the *hatu*.

According to Campbell (1988: 29), rhythmic and melodic aspects of traditional, precontact music were equally important, and performers used a range of percussion instruments and vocal strategies to maintain rhythm. Vocal gesticulations—particularly low-pitched grunts from male performers—referred to by Campbell as *ngau*, or "throat" noises (29)—added to the impact of particularly emotive or "grooving" sections of performance. Hand clapping and body percussion provided further rhythmic accompaniment (Campbell 1988: 30).

TRADITIONAL INSTRUMENTS

All known musical instruments from precontact Rapa Nui were percussive idiophones, used to accompany singing and dancing. While musical instrument development elsewhere in Polynesia was aided by interisland contact (Moyle 1990: 14), Rapa Nui remained outside of these networks until the late nineteenth century. Other than the ceremonial staffs and paddles used in dance routines, it is unclear whether wood was regularly used as a material for making musical instruments on Rapa Nui. Rather, the instruments used by the ancient Rapanui to accompany their singing were crafted from stone.

The most elaborate and unusual of these instruments, the *pukeho*, was a ground drum consisting of two chambers separated by a slate sounding board. To construct the instrument, a waist- or chest-deep pit was dug, wide enough for a person to stand in. A smaller hole was dug into the base of the pit, leaving a rim to support the *keho* (slate). This second hole is reported to have contained a gourd filled with dry grass. The function of the gourd is unknown, though some performers have suggested that it may be a fertility symbol, or that it may have had some sort of acoustic effect.

A special piece of stone was required for the *pukeho*, as Kiko Pate insisted: "it had to be strong enough to support the stamping feet of a grown man, but thin enough to resonate loudly and cleanly" (Luis Pate, personal communication, February 13, 2002). Ideally, a flat piece of slate that was slightly concave on the underside would be chosen for this purpose.

In performance, the *pukeho* would likely have been situated prominently on the performance area. The term *va'e* (Rapanui for "foot" and, more generally, "leg") was used to refer to the designated *pukeho* player, though this role could also be assumed by the *hatu*. The main function of the *pukeho* was to provide a regular beat as an accompaniment to the singing. This was achieved by the *va'e* standing within the *pukeho* and stomping on the slate sounding board. The player's movements were fairly restricted, and the shape and size of the instrument prevented fast-paced rhythms, as too much movement on the part of the *va'e* would muffle the drum. Given the effort and logistics involved in their construction and placement, it is unlikely that *pukeho* were used regularly in performance, and were perhaps reserved only for special occasions.

Different kinds of sounding boards are found throughout Polynesia, but none of them utilize stone and earth in the way that the Rapanui devised, making the *pukeho* quite unique. Contemporary performers have realized this, and some attempts have been made to reincorporate *pukeho* into modern-day performances. For example, in the 2003 Tapati festival traditional song contest, one group of singers dug into the stage area to construct a small version of a *pukeho*. A slate was placed within this hole and struck by a seated performer with a thick stick, providing a high-pitched and distinctly metallic resonance. In other instances, modern *pukeho* have been created from simply placing a piece of slate at ground level, with or without a cavity beneath for resonance.

The second type of instrument associated with ancient Rapanui music is hand-held stone percussion, called *ma'ea poro* (round stone). *Ma'ea poro* stones are found in many places on the Rapa Nui coastline, where hard basalt pieces are washed into smooth, rounded shapes by the sea. Ancient Rapanui musicians used these stones as a rhythmic accompaniment to song and described the instrument in two size categories, using the name *ma'ea poro* for stones that were small enough to be held in the hand and the term *ma'ea haka hetu* for larger *ma'ea poro* that were placed on the ground in front of the performer and struck with a second large stone held between two hands (Loyola 1988: 60).

The different-sized *ma'ea* produce distinct pitches when struck, and the smaller variety can be used to perform very fast-paced rhythms. In a full ensemble context, together with *pukeho*, three distinct rhythmic layers are therefore possible: the fundamental beat of the *pukeho*, a faster beat and/or an off beat executed on the *ma'ea haka hetu*, and a beat at a faster pace issuing from hand-held *ma'ea poro*.

Another instrument associated with traditional performance is the *kauaha*, or horse-jaw rattle, which produces a rattling sound when struck with the hand, causing the teeth within the dried-out jaw to shake. The presence of horses on the island dates back to the 1860s, so it is only after this point in time that the Rapanui started incorporating this instrument into performance, replacing or reinforcing *ma'ea poro* parts. Similar instruments are used in traditional performances in Peru and Chile, and the use of the *kauaha* on Rapa Nui was probably inspired by early contact with the Americas.

Ancient Rapanui performers also knew of, or possessed, conch shells (as observed by Beechey 1831 and asserted by Mètraux 1957: 182). Shells able to be used as aerophones have a number of local names: *pu hura, pipi moroke*, or simply *pu*. The waters around Rapa Nui are outside the natural distribution of the giant conch; however, it is possible that the Rapanui came across conch shells possessed by European explorers, in a similar manner to the introduction of these shells in Aotearoa (Moyle 1990: 39), and that they were subsequently used as signaling devices. Contemporary performers frequently incorporate them into modern-day performances, often played with theatrical gestures to signal the commencement of a song or dance performance.

While conch shells may have been rare on Rapa Nui, the concept of the conch as a signaling device is firmly embedded in Rapanui cultural memory. This is reflected in a unique geocultural feature, the *pu o Hiro*, or "Hiro's trumpet": a meter-high, ovoid rock riddled with natural holes and adorned with many ancient petroglyphs that sits prone on the rocky plain near Hanga o Honu. Hiro is the name of an ancient Rapanui deity, and legend describes the *pu o Hiro* (also sometimes called *ma'ea puhi*, or "wind stone,") as Hiro's own trumpet, able to be sounded by a valiant warrior in the event of approaching enemies (Figure 1.3).

FIGURE 1.3. The *ma'ea puhi*. The stone is represented held aloft on the cover of Kio Teao's 1983 album, *Ka Hoko Mai*. Reproduced with permission.

The channels within the stone do not serve any actual sound-producing function, but the *pu o Hiro* has retained symbolic status as an item possessing magical power. One charismatic political activist once adopted the name of the stone as his own pseudonym, and the celebrated musician Kio Teao once carved himself a smaller version of the *ma'ea puhi* in the shape and size of a conch shell trumpet, which he would wear on a string around his neck and play on special occasions. The cover art for Kio's 1983 studio recording features the performer with traditional tattooing, standing on a rocky outcrop with symbols reminiscent of the ceremonial site at Orongo, holding the immensely heavy *ma'ea puhi* raised to his lips in a display of supernatural *mana*.

OTHER PERFORMANCE
ACCOMPANIMENTS

Throughout Polynesia, song texts are often given physical man-
ifestation through formal dances and movement. As Adrienne
Kaeppler (1980) notes, "dance in Polynesia can be considered as
secondary and tertiary 'decoration' of oral literature" (134). This
description applies to the Rapa Nui context as well. Alongside
hoko, the precontact Rapanui performed vigorous line dances,
or *te ori* (a name for dance borrowed from Tahitian), as well
as more somber, seated or kneeling line dances, where dance
movements and gestures were restricted to the hands, arms,
upper body, and face. The performers of the 1870s also maintained carving practices that enabled the creation of copies of
what had once been ceremonial or ritual objects (staffs, figur-
ines, dancing paddles, and weapons) and worked with *mahute*
(paperbark) fabric, which, while no longer used on a day-to-day
basis due to the importation of Western clothing, was still used
for adornments and items of performance apparel.

Some of the earliest ethnographic descriptions of Rapanui
performance include commentary about local dance practices.
For example, Admiral Abel Aubert Dupetit-Thouars referred
to the dance sketched by Masselot by the name *nagana*, which
McLean (1999) later described as a dance involving "an element
of phallic display" (283). Some years after Dupetit-Thouars,
Knoche described a hopping dance called *katenga* as "a very
obscene dance in which a file of men stand opposite a file of
women . . . [and] consists of jumps on one foot with flexed
knee" (in Mètraux 1940: 359). Meanwhile, Macmillan-Brown
(1926) drew a connection between *hoko* and *'ei* (or as he rendered it, *hei*), describing *'ei* as a genre "sung by men and women
in the hoko-hoko dance" (203). All of these descriptions fall
within the Rapanui understanding of *hoko*, though the genre
has broader applications than just ostentatious display.

Ad Linkels (1999) offered a more nuanced explanation of *hoko*: "to rock the body back and forth while singing" (94), which is applicable to both seated and standing performances. This aligns with a description offered over a century prior by Thompson (1891):

> The peculiar feature of the native dancing is the absence of violent motion; there is no jumping or elaborate pirouettes, no extravagant contortions, and nothing that might be called a precision of step. . . . The feet and hands are kept moving in unison with the slow, monotonous music, while the dancers endeavor to act out the words of the song by pantomime. (469)

Some of the chants and stories preserved in the 1870s came to have *hoko* movements associated with them, and these have subsequently consolidated into a standardized dance repertoire. Meanwhile, contemporary performers have drawn inspiration from historical descriptions of *hoko* dances to develop new, energetic dance sequences to accompany certain chants and ancient texts. *Hoko* therefore has a place alongside 'aparima as a core aspect of ancient performance practice on Rapa Nui.

Ceremonial Objects

Nineteenth-century ethnographic accounts make mention of various carved objects associated with Rapanui ceremonies, and some expeditions collected examples of artifacts including the unique *kohau rongorongo* (wooden tablets containing Rapanui glyphic script). Following the demise of Dutrou-Bornier, the administration of Rapa Nui fell to his former business partners in Tahiti, who sent a representative, Alexander Salmon, to extract what possible benefits may have remained from their Rapa Nui holdings. Salmon helped renew ties to the

Catholic Church and assisted in brokering the contact with Chile that would eventually result in Chile's annexation of the island. He also made practical interventions in the lives of the Rapanui, which included encouraging them to carve replicas of their traditional ceremonial items to trade with visiting merchant ships (McCall 1994: 63). It is possibly due to this influence that a range of ceremonial objects were retained for use in Rapanui performances.

These objects included two kinds of double-ended dancing paddles called *ao* and *rapa* (Mètraux 1940: 209). Handsome examples of these were collected by German and American expeditions in the 1880s and described as being important to traditional ceremonies (Ayres and Ayres 1995: 89–90). The performative function of these paddles is suggested by the fact that they were painted or decorated, often with representations of the deity Makemake. The American collection (located in the National Museum of Natural History) included a paddle-shaped wand carved from whalebone, which is the only one of its kind. The use of dancing paddles in Rapanui performances has been investigated by Adrienne Kaeppler (1998), who described them as being twirled between the palms of seated performers; held at one end between the toes of standing performers who proceed to execute a hopping movement around it; or, alternatively, used in a dance in which "seated men make rowing motions while standing women perform graceful arm and lower-body movements" (952–53).

Another item that occasionally appears in descriptions of early performances is a hoop called a *tekateka* (a term that means "to turn" (*haka tekateka*) or "gyrate"). The hoop was formed from a flexible branch, intersected by two rods forming a cross, and decorated with chicken feathers. Kiko Pate described the *tekateka* as a signaling device used by ensemble leaders in times past.

Other ceremonial items that appear in performance contexts from time to time as adornments include staffs, called *ua*, and chiefly breastplates called *rei miro*. While both of these objects were once restricted to use by chiefs, they no longer have any *tapu* attached to their use and are therefore used quite freely by contemporary performers as symbols of cultural heritage. Campbell also described a lizard or *moko* staff, which, like the other staffs and paddles mentioned previously, could be beaten on the ground as a time-keeping percussion instrument (Campbell 1971: 46), and which also occasionally appears in contemporary performances.

Kai Kai

Like elsewhere in Polynesia, the ancient Rapanui maintained a custom of hand-held string figures, called *kai kai*, that were used to represent some aspects of ancient stories and that may have been mnemonic devices for learning and remembering story texts. Englert interpreted the term *kai kai* as "to show, to elevate on high" (Blixen 1979: 16fn). Mètraux's (1940) informants declared that the string figures served to "memorize popular chants and to recall tales" (354). Some musicians claim that *kai kai* competitions were once a part of ancient ceremonies where children might demonstrate *kai kai* as a kind of public spectacle. *Kai kai* figures are among the best-documented aspects of ancient Rapanui performance culture, with texts such as Isobel Pakarati's (1995: 6) book *Kai Kai* disseminating what would have once been private knowledge, passed down only within the family (Pignet 2001: 375), and other useful descriptions appearing in Campbell (1971) and Blixen (1979). *Kai kai* performances now constitute an important competition category within the annual Tapati Rapa Nui festival.

Costume and Body Decoration

Precontact Rapanui performance practices included a range of corporeal decorations, adornments, and costume items. Feathers from chickens and seabirds—predominantly brown, white, and black in color—were a plentiful resource and could be fashioned into headdresses, tied on long strings to create skirts, or added as an embellishment to other garments (collectively called *haku huruhuru*). Strands of fiber were obtained from *totora* reeds in the island's volcano crater lakes and from the fibrous stalks of banana palms, and these could be used to bind garments together or bunched together to provide body covering (*haku kakaka*). Sheets of cloth were obtained through the hand processing of *mahute* bark from the paper mulberry shrub. This was beaten flat on large stones (a process called *tingitingi mahute*) and then shaped into capes and loincloths (both referred to as *hami*, though this term is now associated principally with the latter). These materials could be painted with natural pigments derived from plants and rocks. As there is no record of when, how, or why such costumes were used in precontact performances, contemporary performers are free to incorporate them at their discretion.

Precontact Rapanui performers also exhibited corporeal decorations in the form of tattooing and *takona* (body painting). Early explorers observed body painting as a part of daily life on Rapa Nui (Arredondo 2004: 70–71) but also noted particular patterns and symbols that were associated with celebration. Contemporary performers maintain the tradition of *takona* in various contexts, including Tapati Rapa Nui, where a competition category exists for traditional body painting. Stone, ash, and plant extracts provided pigments of red, yellow, orange, black, and white that could be used for *takona*. As described by Arredondo (2004), the ancient Rapanui perfected methods of preserving and transporting *takona* paints, using sugar cane juice and saliva as binding agents for the powdered pigments.

TRADITIONAL CHANTS AND SONGS

Despite the considerable cultural loss caused by the slave raids of the 1860s (Porteous 1981), the Rapanui of the 1870s preserved songs and musical practices that suggest the existence of a coherent and distinctive musical system. Different aspects of this ancient knowledge appear in the various music studies produced over the course of the last century (especially Pereira Salas 1947; Urrutia Blondel 1958; Campbell 1971; Loyola 1988; Abarca 2015). Medical doctor Ramón Campbell's (1971) book *La Herencia musical de Rapanui*, which was the product of two years of doctoral research in the 1960s, and which is possibly the first example of Chilean scholarship to be described as an "ethnomusicology," is the most detailed of these works.

Campbell's research was pivotal to fostering awareness of Rapanui music and culture in mainland Chile and the rest of the world. However, he devised his own taxonomy of genres and style definitions in his attempt to interpret the songs that he collected, transcribed, and translated, leading to some confusing classifications that do not necessarily reflect Rapanui traditional knowledge. Much of the available information about Rapanui music in the public domain (e.g., McLean 1999; Kaeppler and Gonzalez 1998) reflects Campbell's important work but lacks an indigenous perspective. Abarca's (2015) *Riu, el canto primal de Rapa Nui* redresses this imbalance somewhat, as the book is almost entirely based on the musical knowledge and memories of elder Maria Elena Hotu. The discussion that follows attempts to advance this perspective further.

From an indigenous perspective, the singular most important element of the songs and chants preserved by the Rapanui of the 1870s is the text. Like other Polynesians (see Moyle 1991: 5), the ancient Rapanui believed in the power of the spoken, chanted, or sung word to imbue a performance with meaning. The chants and song texts preserved in the late nineteenth century drew their textual content from four main sources of inspiration: stories concerning Rapanui ancient history (called a'amu tuai), references to the supernatural world, references to the natural world, and references to significant contemporary events or individuals.

The first of these four domains is primarily concerned with references to the Rapa Nui foundation story and reverence for the founding monarch Hotu Matu'a. The second includes depictions of supernatural events described in Rapanui myths, as well as references to deities and ancestor spirits, or aku aku. Ramón Campbell collected so many examples of these that he proposed aku aku as a discrete song genre, though this is not how his informants would have described them. The third domain includes references to landmarks and ancestral lands, as well as references to fauna that were important to precontact Rapanui life. The fourth domain, contemporary events and people, indicates a role for formal performance as a means of chronicling events within living memory, for the purposes of posterity.

A well-crafted recitation could convey overt and covert messages, and lyrical prowess was a means by which a presenter's mana (influence or power) could be ascertained. Metaphors and symbolic references were a feature of ancient Rapanui texts, and the use of metaphor helped to convey embedded or restricted messages in Rapanui performances on various levels. In his analysis of ancient chants, Thomas Barthel (1978) suggested four levels of meaning that may be present in any poetic text: naturalistic description, comparison with a similar action in a different environment, transference to sexual behavior and frustration, and the elevation of biological events to a mythological plane (170). Sometimes these texts were structured as extended narratives or recitations (*te ako*). At other times they were transformed into rhythmic chants and song texts, as described next.

RITUAL CHANTS, LINEAGE CHANTS, AND *PATAUTAU*

Of the various ritual chants that likely existed in precontact Rapanui culture, only one example was retained beyond the 1860s: the rain-making chant, *aro ki te ua,* which was recounted to ethnographers who visited Rapa Nui in the early twentieth century (Figure 1.4). In one account, prominent elder Juan Tepano described the purpose of this ritual to priest (and ethnographer) Sebastian Englert as follows:

> The man in charge of the prayers would go down to the sea to get coral stones, called karakamá, as well as seaweed. Alone, he would climb a hill. But he would leave the stones below, at the foot of the hill. Arriving on top he would say [chant] this prayer. . . . Later, the prayer man would come down to the sweet potato, banana,

E te u-a ma-ta-vai ro-a a Hi-ro e_____

ka ho-a mai ko-e ki-ra-ro

FIGURE 1.4. The chant for making rain (*Aro ki te ua*). The invocation calls upon the god Hiro to cry big tears (*matavai roa*) over the land.

and yam plantings. He would take the stones and seaweed and put them into the ground. Then it would rain. (Englert 2002: 33)

While this chant was not used in a ritual context beyond the 1880s, respected elder Kiko Pate claimed to have been taught a version of it in his youth. His rendition featured a loose binary pulse accented on the beat, with a slight rise in pitch to convey emphasis on the name of the deity Hiro.

Like elsewhere in Polynesia, chants also played a role in the mediation of formal social relationships in precontact Rapanui—a hierarchical society with strict social protocols. While no examples of such interactions were ever recorded, Kiko Pate believed that lineage chants, which he called *hui tupuna, manu tupuna,* or simply *manu,* were used as a mode of social engagement, and possibly as a way of negotiating status and relationships with others. The importance of genealogy to the ancient Rapanui is reflected in Fischer's assertion that the *rongo rongo* script on the famous Santiago Staff represents a list of family lineage (Flenley and Bahn 2003: 189), which may have had some sort of formal function. However, where Fisher's genealogy is marked by phallic glyphs separating the name of each ancestor, the *manu tupuna* preserved by Kiko Pate had a matrilineal emphasis (Figure 1.5).

All of the ancestors named in this chant belong to the Tupa Hotu clan, with verses two and three pertaining to the ancestors of the Pakarati family, and verse four pertaining to the ancestors of the Pate family. According to Pate, this indicated a historical association between these clan groups. The final section of the recitation calls forth the ancestors as a kind of spiritual vanguard, supporting the singer. Pate claimed to have learned this chant from Arturo Teao, who accompanied his rendition with vigorous hand gestures indicating where the guardians were placed: to the front, to the back, and to both sides.

E pu e pu heneke e te pu	From this womb
Piri vaenga no mai	Coming together here (in the middle)
Ia Maherenga te ono	The six (children) of Maherenga
Kia ia	Who are they?
Kia Tepihi Va'e Rei	They are Tepihi, Va'e Rei
Ma'unga Teatea	(And) Ma'unga Teatea
Kia ia te ono	These are they
Kia ia	Who are they?
Kia Ku ki Arava kai te ono	They are Ku, Arava
Ke te Vero o te ko Hou	Vero and Hou
A te Matangi	And Matangi
A ure te ono	These are the generations
Kia ia	Who are they?
Ki te Manu Rangaranga Vai	Manu Rangaranga Vai
A Maherenga te ono	Of Maherenga
Mai taki koe	Come here, guard
Tou aro e	To my front
Tou tu'a e	Behind me
Tou kaukau e	And to both sides
Ho'i riva e	This is assuredly great
Manu riva e	This *manu*
Piu riva e	Very great

FIGURE 1.5. An example of *manu tupuna*. Kiko Pate's version of a Pate and Pakarati family lineage chant.

Patautau

Poetic chants, collectively called *patautau* (a term likely borrowed from the Tahitian *pata'uta'u*), constitute the main body of chant repertoire to have been preserved from precontact times. There are around two dozen remnant examples of *patautau*, ranging from ten to fifty or more lines in length. Their topics vary widely, from depictions of ancient battles to descriptions of navigation. Most contain words that are obsolete and phrases that are esoteric, or which convey metaphors that can no longer be understood. In some cases, the meaning of a text might only be guessed at, originally known only to a select few (Barthel 1978: 171–72), while in others it more clearly relates to a historical event or some other practical aspect of historical social life.

In their important collections, both Mètraux and Routledge positioned the *patautau* chants they gathered as "oral history," without considering them as performance items. Ramón Campbell's 1971 book contains transcriptions of eleven *patautau*, with rhythmic transcription for ten of them (394–412, 434), as preserved by nineteenth-century performers and passed down through oral transmission to their descendants. Campbell suggested a connection between *patautau* recitations and the interpretation of *kohau rongorongo*, the "talking boards" that contain all known examples of ancient Rapanui script, though this has not been substantiated.

Patautau *Performance*

Unlike the two examples of ceremonial chant described earlier, *patautau* are performed with a marked binary meter, accompanied by choreographed gestures and, in some cases, *kai kai* string figures depict elements of the narrative. An instructive example is the *patautau* "Kaunga te Rongo," which relates an esoteric dialogue between various protagonists that culminates with a depiction of sexual congress. The chant is performed in even four-beat phrases (Figure 1.6).

A consistent rhythmic unit consisting of four eighth notes followed by two quarter notes is maintained through most of this *patautau*, except for a few short breaks that appear at the end of larger phrases, timed so that the next phrase can commence without disrupting the rhythm of the subsequent unit.

Similarly, the Hetereki *patuatu*, named after the warrior whose apocryphal battle it recounts, also maintains a quadratic meter throughout. The Hetereki *patautau* is considered historical, insofar as the battle it describes and the protagonists

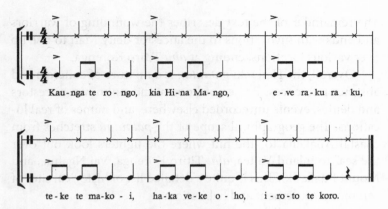

FIGURE 1.6. *Kaunga te rongo.* The first phrase of this *patautau*, with indicative rhythmic patterns.

He ika uru atua ratena	The victims, with god within them, are
Ko Eho ko Mahorangi	Eho and Mahorangi
Ko Rangi Heturu ko Puku Pati	Rangi Heturu and Puku Pati
Ko te nuahine	And the old lady (Renga Miti Miti)
Huri tau'a a Ta'ereka	Turns the battle in favour of Ta'ereka
Kahuira ka huri a	Quickly, like a lightning bolt, return
Te tau'a nei e	Now, fighters
E Renga Miti Miti a Vai e	Oh, Renga Miti Miti, daughter of Vai
Mai varavara	Come here, disband
Mai takitaki	Come here, disperse
Mai takaure tua	Here, like flies
Te huka o te tau'a...	The rearguard of fighters...

FIGURE 1.7. The *Hetereki patautau.* The first section of the text.

named are understood to have been real people. The extract provided in Figure 1.7 begins by naming the key individuals involved in the story: soon-to-be-vanquished warriors (the *ika*, or victims) Eho, Mahorangi, Rangi Heturu, and Puku Pati, as well as the "old lady" *tumu ivi atua* (a shaman or "witch") Renga Miti Miti a Vai and her patron Ta'ereka. At the fourth line, the chant depicts the intervention of Renga Mitimiti a Vai, "turning the battle" in favor of warrior Ta'ereka (Zamora and Rapu 1995: 48).

The remainder of the text describes the wounding of warriors and ends with invocations to the ancestor deity Mati to rise up over various locations, ending at *ahu* Titiro Korenga.

Overall, the Hetereki *patautau* is a mixture of concrete and abstract references: names of known and unknown ancestors and deities, events unrecorded elsewhere, and names of real locations. The geographical scope of the *patautau* stretches from coastal Anakena to "the hill where the fighters look out over the sea" to inland Vaitea, *ahu* Titiro Korenga, Vai Ngahue, and Mount Puakatiki. This is quite a detailed list of historical sites of ceremony, settlement and habitation.

Another well-known *patautau, Ka tere te vaka* ("maneuver the boat"), recounts a sailing expedition in the region of Akahanga (Figure 1.8). In this case, the text is not making supernatural or historical references so much as setting out navigational instructions. The literalness of this particular *patautau* makes it a very popular recitation with contemporary performers. It is also accompanied by one of the easier *kai kai* string figures, which has a large inverse triangle that represents the hull of a boat. It has also been popular as a source for short songs based on fragments of the full *patautau* text. These have been incorporated into at least two songs venerating Hotu Matu'a, which are themselves regarded as "traditional."

Ka tere te vaka	Manoeuvre the boat
O Akahanga	Through Akahanga
Ka mimiro te vaka	Turn the boat
O Huareva	At Huareva
Ka tere te tere	This is the way
Ko Ure Roverove	Of Ure Roverove
A Hare'o Ave	Son of Hare'o Ave
Ka ngaro ro ki hiva	(Who was) lost to Hiva

FIGURE 1.8. *Ka tere te vaka.*

ANCIENT SONGS AND SINGING

Alongside the chant repertoire, the Rapanui performers of the late nineteenth century also preserved a repertoire of songs, collectively called *riu*, that together constitute a unique knowledge base. The term *riu* can be understood to apply to all Rapanui songs, though in practice it is mainly used in reference to repertoire that emanates from the nineteenth century or to more recent songs that preserve "traditional" texts or musical expressions. Contemporary Rapanui musicians sometimes substitute the Tahitian words *himene* (derived from "hymn") or *himene api* ("new" *himene*) to refer to songs composed more recently or to their own compositions.

Befitting the primacy of the text in ancient Rapanui music, *riu* are best understood when considered in terms of their function or textual emphasis. Based on this approach, Abarca (2015) identified twenty-nine different types (or genres) of *riu*. However, some of these overlap or fulfill very similar social functions. If considered as a group, the songs retained from precontact times (as well as those preserved from the late nineteenth and early twentieth centuries that are considered "traditional") fall into three main types: laments, songs of celebration or gratitude, and songs of insult or ridicule.

LAMENTS

The largest body of extant *riu* are *riu tangi*, literally "sad" songs, or crying songs (Hotus et al. 2000: 171). *Riu tangi* have also been described as sentimental or erotic songs (Englert 1995: 235), lamentations (Pereira Salas 1947: 7), or more specifically funeral laments (Mètraux 1940: 355). Their prevalence in the traditional repertoire perhaps provides another explanation for Loti's description of the "gloomy" music he encountered on Rapa Nui. Scholars with knowledge of New Zealand Māori music have noted the functional similarity of *riu tangi* to Māori *tangi* (McLean 1999: 286; Felbermayer 1972: 270); however, *riu tangi* are not "funeral songs" by definition, as they have a range of other functions.

A more inclusive understanding of this category of song would be to describe *riu tangi* as songs expressing strong emotion, including grief and nostalgia, within which lamentations figure substantially, but which could also include songs expressing anger, pride, disgust, or other strong emotions. As reflected in Abarca (2015), some Rapanui musicians advocate for more specific descriptions of *riu* or *riu tangi* that deal with particular emotions. These include *riu ture* (songs of justice or solidarity), *riu mo te tane mate* (funeral laments), and *riu tangi ora mo te matu'a* (songs to honor one's father). Songs that convey a happy story, beautiful songs, and songs that are otherwise deemed to have "good" topics may be described as *riu reka*.

SONGS OF CELEBRATION AND GRATITUDE

Alongside *riu tangi*, the ancient Rapanui had various names for songs that were intended for celebration or to express gratitude. One term readily encountered in the literature dating back to the 1880s, but rarely used since then, is *ate*, which was applied to songs with specific honorific functions. Paloma Huke (1995) defined *ate* as songs of worship, dedicated to important historical individuals or events (34), and some religious songs, including songs associated with Catholic worship, are referred to as *ate atua*. Campbell (1971) regarded *ate atua* as "songs to honor a king or leader" (288), while Englert (1995) listed *ate atua* as one of the three kinds of songs used in *koro* celebrations

(231) and described them as "songs of praise" (232). Two other types of *ate, ate manava mate* and *ate manava more*, could be described as "love songs," where the singer is expressing some element of romantic love or, in the case of *ate manava more*, nostalgia.

With a similarly honorific function to *ate, hakakio* songs are those that are sung in an expression of tribute, described as a "repayment of attentions" (Englert 1995: 235). The social enactment of *hakakio* probably relates to the *koro paina* festivals described earlier, as these celebrations often revolved around public expressions of gratitude.

SONGS OF INSULT OR RIDICULE

Where tribute and thanksgiving were important contexts for musical creation, the ancient Rapanui invested similar creative energy in dueling songs, songs of ridicule (*haka me'eme'e*), and slander (*haka kakata*), collectively called *'ei*. Both Mètraux (1940: 179) and Felbermayer (1972) describe *'ei* as songs of satirical intent, while Englert (1995: 237) described them as *kupu rakerake* ("bad mouth" recitations) and stated that they were devised carefully, long in advance of the performance event. Campbell (1971: 323–24) stated that song battles were sometimes organized by disputing clans or individuals wishing to articulate or settle a dispute, a notion echoed by contemporary culture bearer Antonio Tepano Hito when reflecting on the situation of his forefathers:

> In those days, you could kill a man for the slightest transgression. Any insult was a call to war. But if you did it in song, you could say anything because the only way to respond was with another *'ei*. The most skillful song would be the winner. (Antonio Tepano Hito, personal communication, May 20, 2003)

E uka nui nui, by Juan Tepano, sung to curse Verónica Mahute:

E uka nui nui o ahu e	Big woman from near the ahu
Ka puha to'u mata i te roe	May the ants sting your eyes
E ko hoki atu ta taura renga	You won't achieve your goals
Te paina ina tuhi renga	Your 'festival of presentation'

Verónica Mahute's response to Juan Tepano, *I te po te to'a*:

I te po te to'a ko Ure Henguh engu	At night, your enemy Ure Henguhengu
Ei hao hao mai nei	Is setting up a curse for you
He'i ma oa oa haka ou mai koe	He's opening that which should not be opened
I te umu oma ana kio	The ground-oven of Ana Kio
Airoto e tangi	You feel pain
E tavi taviri era	Turning around in
Te nui tangata hare	The 'big man's' house

FIGURE 1.9. *E uka nui nui* and *I te po te to'a*. These two songs formed part of a memorable *'ei* battle in 1922, as recounted by Kiko Pate.

An example of this can be seen in a song battle from 1922, in which Juan Tepano composed an *'ei* against Verónica Mahute, who skillfully responded by mimicking his song form and singing it back at him, shown in Figure 1.9.

In both of these songs, the specific reason for the curse is never stated directly, though it is likely that each performer knew what the other was referring to, and both are overtly threatening. It was also quite common for *'ei* such as these to have movements acted out in performance, making some veiled references more explicit.

PERFORMING *RIU*

With the exception of one particular genre called *riu tuai* (discussed later), *riu* did not have any restrictions regarding their composition. In practice, most extant *riu* are strophic, mostly with a binary pulse, with texts treated syllabically and divided into eight-beat phrases of even length. Some incorporate melodic material drawn from contemporary sources, such as religious songs, that began filtering into Rapanui performances from the 1860s onward. Specific melodies that were very popular were often remembered and reworked into new compositions, resulting in a repertoire that, to nineteenth-century European ears, unable to understand the textual differences, might have seemed repetitive. The extant repertoire of *riu* contains clusters of similar-sounding songs alongside songs with melodies that diverge in any possible direction. *Riu*, on the whole, therefore resist categorization by musical characteristics alone.

The ability to improvise (*haka kakati*) new song texts or to branch out (*haka manga*) to create new songs inspired by old ones appears to have been central to precontact Rapanui music making and was remarked upon in early twentieth-century ethnographic accounts (Mètraux 1940: 358; Estella 1920). Reverend Father Bienvenido de Estella (1920), who visited Rapa Nui between 1918 and 1920, was particularly impressed with the ability of children to create songs on impulse (Figure 1.10):

> See, for example the song "Eme ore ore tote Capuchine," which the older schoolboys and schoolgirls invented before my very own beard as they were leaving the school, going to the mission as

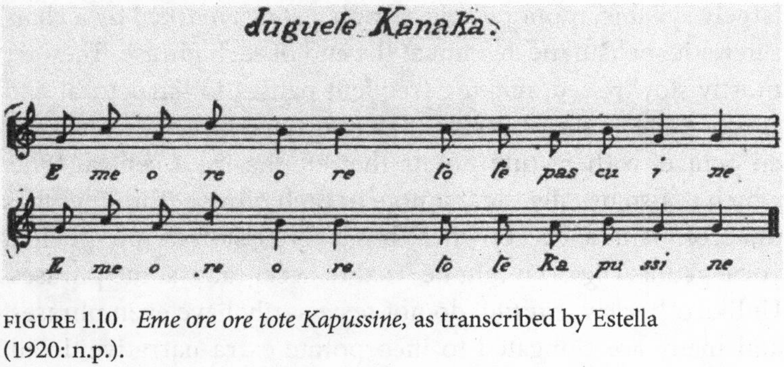

FIGURE 1.10. *Eme ore ore tote Kapussine,* as transcribed by Estella (1920: n.p.).

they were accustomed to do. They went all together in one group; I was just returning from a study-walk along the beach, and was returning to the mission myself. The boys and girls surrounded me as they were accustomed to do, and, with a playful spirit, began their song, playing on the words reo-reo, ore-ore, liar, liar, directed at me, as a kind reproach because I tricked them with offers of sweets which I then never gave them.... Admiring their verses, completely new to me, I said: Who has taught you this song? - Ourselves, they replied with satisfaction. Doubting this, I approached some of the more learned Pascuans and asked them if they had ever heard this song before, to which they replied: No, father, the kids have just invented it now; don't be surprised, our people always invent lots of things. (76–77)

Riu Tuai

The one genre of *riu* to possess a defined musical form is called *riu tuai* ("old" or "ancient" songs). *Riu tuai* are considered by contemporary Rapanui performers to be their most culturally significant ancient song genre. They are musically distinguished by a specific melodic structure held to be very ancient by Rapanui performers. This melodic form is depicted, though not identified by name, in various historical accounts.

Sung by individuals or in small ensembles, *riu tuai* are largely syllabic, monophonic, strophic songs marked by a characteristic melismatic descent at the end of each phrase. They are mostly slow paced, making frequent pauses for structural and emotive effect. They extend over a range that is rarely wider than an octave, with resting points that emphasize a central tone, which is also usually the last note in each phrase. The singing is unaccompanied, except where basic percussion or low-pitched vocal grunts (*ngau*) might be used to accentuate some phrases. Unlike other *riu, riu tuai* do not necessarily have even phrases, and many are elongated to incorporate extra narrative detail.

The pulse and tempo in *riu tuai* may sometimes be guided by the rhythm of the text rather than a fixed meter.

Songs matching this description have a long history on Rapa Nui. For Pierre Loti, *riu tuai* were at the forefront of the music he encountered:

> They sing, the Maoris; they all sing, banging their hands to mark a dance rhythm. The women give sweet notes. . . The men produce notes with a deep cavernous sound. Their music is composed of short phrases, ending in lugubrious vocal descents, in the minor mode. (Loti 1988 [1899]: 85)

For Pacific anthropologist John Macmillan-Brown (1926), the singing was "monotonous, generally consisting in the repetition of a word or phrase" (202–3). However, for Bienvenido de Estella (1920), the sound of *riu tuai* resembled something more akin to Gregorian chant: "I sense a strong flavor of plainchant, even Gregorian chant in some of them, but nothing resembling known examples" (75).

Writing toward the middle of the twentieth century, Chilean musicologist Jorge Urrutia Blondel (1958) astutely noted that some old Rapanui songs seemed to possess a distinctive "topography" with a particular kind of descending melisma at the end of the phrase (38). Ramón Campbell (1971) found this to be such a prominent aspect of the music that he dedicated a section of his analysis to "beginnings and endings" of songs, though he did not go into much further categorization other than to simply describe these songs as being "ancient" (77).

Each phrase in a *riu tuai* is accompanied by a refrain that serves to recap the topic of the song and emphasize a key message. The phrase usually has a melody line that moves toward or revolves around a "central tone" (tonic) before descending toward the same tone an octave below at the end of the phrase (if a phrase dips too low, the performer may transpose the ending back to the upper octave). This gesture is balanced by a refrain that reworks some aspect of the phrase and then adds a melismatic fragment that functions as the phrase ending, which may occur over a single elongated vocable or may contain some text.

The widely documented *riu tangi Ka hi a Manu* provides a typical example of *riu tuai* song form. In this case, the tonic is not established until the name Manu is articulated with a distinctive glissando. Upon reaching this point, the pace of the phrase is slowed so as to emphasize the dominant-tonic shift (Figure 1.11).

In Figure 1.11, the tonic (B flat) does not appear until the end of the phrase but is set up by the melodic movement on either side (from the sixth to the upper second scale degrees). This tonic is then confirmed by the use of a stereotypical *riu tuai* melisma, running from a third above the tonic through to a pause that accentuates the dominant (fifth scale degree) and ending on the lower octave of the tonic (Figure 1.12).

Every time that this melisma is repeated, it further reinforces the tonic, providing resting points between phrases

Ka pa - ri   mai   tou,   to - to ha - re ki - ri au   i   te po,   e Ma -   nu e...

FIGURE 1.11. *Ka hi a Manu.* The first phrase of *Ka hi a Manu*, which demonstrates the typical *riu tuai* melodic form, which Estella (1920) compared to Gregorian chant.

e - e   -   e   -   -   e

FIGURE 1.12. *Ka hi a Manu,* melismatic phrase ending.

and a clear endpoint for each. While the exact form, duration, and associated text of this melismatic passage may vary from verse to verse even within the same song, the general contour is maintained, as is its function as an endpoint to melodic phrases.

As a further feature, some *riu tuai* end with a coda, which summarizes the song subject and/or provides some detail about the song's provenance. This coda is sung a minor third (or thereabouts) below the central tone but ends with the same melismatic descent that characterizes the verses, returning to the tonic at the end of the song.

SINGING, SURVIVING

The song styles, musical concepts, accompaniments, and performance practices described in this chapter constitute the legacy of precontact Rapanui music, as preserved in the 1870s by a community of just over a hundred people. Undoubtedly, the social change wrought by foreign incursions into Rapa Nui in the 1860s and 1870s resulted in the loss of a great deal of traditional musical knowledge; however, it is remarkable to consider how much knowledge survived to be passed down to subsequent generations.

The ethnographic record demonstrates not only that performers were persisting with some precontact musical practices but also that many of these practices were still part of a living culture well into the twentieth century. Some of them have never receded: for example, most contemporary performance ensembles still organize around a dominant leader (a *hatu*), *riu* of all kinds have continued to be composed throughout the twentieth century, and traditional musical instruments appear alongside introduced ones in modern performances. As the following chapters will reveal, performance practices associated with obsolete or discontinued ceremonies and ritual did not entirely disappear. Rather, they were gradually incorporated into other types of public celebration including Catholic rituals, marriage celebrations, civic events, tourist shows, and, ultimately, the island's annual cultural festival, Tapati Rapa Nui.

2

RELIGION AND RENEWAL

> The people who sing this music are not savages, but
> quite cultured. . . . Europeans themselves would have
> wished for something similar to this truly religious and
> ultra-Gregorian hymn.
>
> —TOMAS DE LLAVALLOL *commenting on Rapanui music*
> *transcriptions sent by his friend and colleague Reverend Father*
> *Bienvendio de Estella (in Estella 1920: 76)*

REVEREND FATHER BIENVENDIO DE ESTELLA was one of a succession of Chilean Catholic priests to be dispatched to Rapa Nui in the early twentieth century. Following Chilean annexation in 1888, Rapa Nui was brought under provincial jurisdiction of the Quinta Región of Chile. The spiritual well-being of the Rapanui people became the responsibility of the Valparaíso diocese, which maintained a sparse roster of priestly visits to this geographically isolated island. Arriving in 1918, Estella had little way of knowing what to expect from his visit to Rapa Nui, other than a routine schedule of marriages, baptisms and Masses that any itinerant priest might be required to perform. As far as he knew, he was being sent to the most remote outpost of the Chilean state, inhabited by a people who shared no obvious affinity with Chile other than their colonial status and religious adherence.

It must have been quite remarkable, after more than a week at sea, for Estella to discover a small community rich in cultural heritage and keen to engage with him on every social and spiritual level. Estella's gleeful surprise at the richness of Rapanui culture imbues every page of the book he wrote upon his return to Chile (Estella 1920). Where music is concerned, Estella luxuriated in his Rapanui musical experiences, transcribing a selection of songs, and becoming the first outsider to set Rapanui songs to Western notation. He was convinced of the richness of this musical culture, that it must stand as evidence of a highly developed society, and sought confirmation of this from a friend in Argentina, Tomas de Llavallol, whom he considered to be the highest musical authority that he knew. Llavallol's correspondence with Estella provided this confirmation, favorably comparing *riu* with Gregorian chant.

Estella was not the first (and certainly not the last) visitor to marvel at the music of the Rapanui, which he framed as evidence of their godliness. From the 1860s onward, much Rapanui music, whether sacred or secular, had begun to include elements of Catholic Church music, which was a generative force in the post-1860s reconstruction of Rapanui culture. Throughout the twentieth century, the church provided a focal point for community gatherings, a context in which indigenous leadership was encouraged, and a vehicle for finding common ground and brokering interactions with outsiders. The adoption of Catholic worship practices also fostered new song repertoires and musical ideas in Rapanui culture, including the Rapa Nui Mass, and other influences that have permeated Rapanui performance culture more broadly. This chapter explores the Catholic Church's contribution to Rapanui musical heritage, from the actions and observations of early missionaries through to the development of distinctive sacred music on Rapa Nui in the mid-twentieth century.

The concept of an omnipotent, transcendent God existed in Rapanui culture prior to the arrival of missionaries in the form of ancestral deity Makemake, whose face is symbolically represented in petroglyphs and carvings across the island. However, the early success of the Sacred Heart mission owes as much to the particular historical circumstances of the island in the 1860s as it does to any shared religious concepts. In the aftermath of the social upheaval and population decline stemming from the "blackbirding" raids of the 1860s, the arrival of the missionaries marked a new period for Rapanui interaction with the outside world. Never before had outsiders arrived with the intention of remaining on Rapa Nui. Furthermore, the missionaries introduced a schedule of ritual practices revolving around congregational singing, which likely proved attractive to many Rapanui. Music provided the Church with a foothold in Rapa Nui, and the music of the Church in turn provided inspiration for the development and expansion of Rapanui performance practices.

The position and influence of the Catholic Church, and of Catholicism as a majority religion, is not uncontested on Rapa Nui. Some Rapanui maintain that their forebears' acceptance and adaptation of Catholicism is regrettable, that the Church was antithetical to Rapanui traditional culture, and that the enduring cultural position of the Church should be questioned. Chilean historian Castro Flores (2006) provides an elegant description of the Rapa Nui Sacred Heart mission as a fundamentally destructive project that sought to rid the Rapanui of the pagan practices of their ancestors. However, for better or worse, the Church became and remains a significant element in the social lives of numerous generations of Rapanui, and the enduring influence of Catholic Church practices in Rapanui music is something that can't be ignored.

In accepting Catholicism in the 1860s, the Rapanui benefited from new pathways for interaction with French Polynesia, on the one hand, and Chile on the other. Many contemporary Rapanui culture bearers consider their Tahiti-derived hymn repertoires as inseparable from other ancient traditions and do not necessarily regard this music, or indeed the Church itself, as a "foreign" influence. Furthermore, on a handful of well-documented occasions, the Church actively supported indigenous social and cultural causes, sometimes against the will of the island's Chilean administration. Finally, through the adoption of Tahitian hymn repertoire, Rapanui performers developed a way to communicate with other Polynesians who share Christian hymn–derived song repertoires and thereby established a platform for the reification of their own Pacific cultural identity in contemporary trans-Pacific contexts.

Some writers on Rapanui music (McLean 1999; Loyola 1988) dismiss Rapanui Christian music as an acculturated Western cultural influence relevant mainly to worship contexts. However, Christian hymnody has also had an audible impact on secular Rapanui music, influencing the harmonic and melodic sensibilities of Rapanui music and providing an array of useful new techniques and concepts that were woven into Rapanui music throughout the twentieth century. Meanwhile, the ritual calendar of Catholic festivals and activities became a vehicle for some aspects of traditional Rapanui ritual practice that were otherwise declining in secular contexts. Those families that remained closest to the Church have maintained a cycle of hereditary responsibility for religious events, in turn planting and harvesting crops that support the Church's activities throughout the year, in a similar way to how ancient Rapanui communities once managed their own cycles of interclan tribute and hospitality.

The Sacred Hearts were not the only religious order to reach Rapa Nui, though their enduring influence is unquestionable, supported in part by historical legacy but also by the ubiquity of the Catholic Church in Chile. Other religious orders that can be found on Rapa Nui include Mormons, Jehovah's Witnesses, and Seventh Day Adventists. However, these congregations are much smaller, sometimes consisting of extended family groups or just individual families. The community's religious needs past and present are otherwise served entirely by the Catholic

Church, the Harepure Tepito te Henua, which is the focus of this chapter.

THE RAPA NUI MISSION

The impact of the Pacific slave trade of the 1860s, so disastrous for Rapa Nui, was also felt in Tahiti, where Bishop Stephan "Tépano" Jaussen actively petitioned the French government to exert pressure on Peru to put an end to it. Jaussen assisted in the repatriation of transported Polynesians, including the Rapanui, who were returned to their island in the company of a French lay preacher, Eugene Eyraud. Eyraud had received some of his religious education in South America, was aware of Rapa Nui, and had volunteered to initiate a mission there. He was the first foreigner to spend any significant length of time on the island, completing an initial stay of about nine months.

Eyraud encountered a society in reconstruction, with new clan leaders vying for political supremacy. An *ariki* named Torometi saw Eyraud's arrival as an opportunity for demonstrating his own *mana* to the population of the Hangaroa sector where Eyraud had landed. Torometi allowed the missionary to build a small house on land at Apina Nui, perhaps unaware that this would be interpreted by Torometi as acceptance of his overlordship (Englert 1964: 25). Eyraud was subsequently stripped of his possessions and had his movements closely controlled. Nevertheless, his experiences living among Torometi's people gave him unprecedented insight into their culture. Eyraud was released from his captivity when a ship sailing under the direction of the Valparaiso Sacred Hearts arrived at Hangaroa late in 1864. He boarded and then remained in Chile for a year before finding an opportunity to return to Rapa Nui and complete his mission, buoyed by sponsorship and support from the Church and the wider Valparaiso community.

In 1866, Eyraud traveled to Papeete and then to Rapa Nui with the assistance of two more experienced missionaries from Valparaiso and Mangareva, as well as three Mangarevan volunteers who, it was hoped, would be readily welcomed by the Rapanui (Englert 1964: 37–38). Reverend Father Hyppolyte Roussel had spent some years in the Tuamotu Islands, where he learned the local language (*te re'o pa'umotu*), and this was similar enough to the Rapanui language that he was able to communicate effectively with the Rapanui. Thus reinforced, Eyraud soon established a chapel on the site of the current church in Hangaroa and began to observe Mass. The other missionaries went on to establish a second mission at Vaihu, the site of another hamlet. On February 14, 1868, the missionaries baptized 380 adult converts to Christianity.

The Mass proved popular as entertainment, and Eyraud quickly developed a regular audience observing and participating in his ministrations. While the Latin words of the liturgy were incomprehensible to the Rapanui, they could nevertheless recognize the ritual character of the Mass and could appreciate its musical flavor, particularly the *riu tuai* qualities of liturgical chant. Ramón Campbell speculated that Eyraud may also have sung nonliturgical hymns in French, and Reverend Father Bienvenido de Estella (1920: 76) transcribed at least one religious song sung by the Rapanui in the 1920s that he considered to be based on a French melody.

Eyraud died in 1868, but the mission continued for another two years, until pressure from an ascendant Dutrou-Bornier, in his attempts to exert complete control over Rapa Nui, finally led to the evacuation of the missionaries and many of their disciples to French Polynesia. Between 1870 and 1888, Rapa Nui remained under the broad mandate of the Papeete diocese in Tahiti, though the Church intervened little in Rapa Nui affairs until after Dutrou-Bornier's death. The vulnerability of Rapa Nui to further exploitation was a concern for the

Tahitian bishop, who, together with his Chilean counterparts, encouraged Chile's growing interest in claiming Rapa Nui in the 1880s. Indeed, Church representatives were sent to Rapa Nui in the lead-up to Chile's act of annexation in 1888, ostensibly on routine visits, but also seeking to prepare the population for Chilean annexation, with the promise that this would provide more stable religious services for Rapa Nui (Englert 1964: 65). However, the appointment of a permanent parish priest would not occur until 1937. In the interim, the Church tended to the spiritual needs of the Rapanui by training and appointing an indigenous lay preacher, Ure Potahi, whose life and work was the first phase in the consolidation of an indigenous Rapanui Catholic faith.

INDIGENIZING THE CHURCH

Ure Potahi a Te Pihi (or Nicolás Pakarati, as he would later be known) was a Rapanui man who had grown up in the embrace of the Tahitian missionaries. He was one of the few Rapanui to continue to observe religious services after the closure of the mission in 1871. In 1886 his efforts were rewarded with an invitation to travel to Mangareva for religious instruction. Here he was christened with the name Panakarati, which was later shortened to Pakarati, and married Elisabet Ranguitaki, a Mangarevan woman. After the Chilean annexation of 1888, the Pakarati couple were dispatched back to Rapa Nui by the Church, with the aim of reviving the Rapa Nui mission. Pakarati established himself on what remained of the mission property at Hangaroa and, together with Elisabet (called Isapera on Rapa Nui, and affectionately known as "Sape"), resumed the Church's activities.

Pakarati was an inspired choice as leader for the revival of the Rapa Nui mission. He was an indigenous man with direct experience with both Chile and French Polynesia, who could converse in Tahitian, French, and Spanish and possessed a strong devotion to the Church. Though his wife was new to Rapanui, she quickly established a social position as her husband's assistant in Church matters, and she became a conduit for widespread community engagement with the Church through the medium of song. Sape made a point of getting to know everyone in her new community by moving from dwelling to dwelling and spending a night with each family. Kiko Pate recalled that she would arrive before sunset and, once introduced to all family members, would begin to sing hymn songs in Tahitian and teach them to family members in the domestic setting, often continuing late into the night.

Nicolás Pakarati consolidated this work by introducing the same songs to Saturday choral rehearsals in both Hangaroa and Vaihu (Englert 1964: 68). Tahitian and Rapanui languages are not identical, but they do share enough common words so as to be largely mutually intelligible, especially within the thematic scope of hymn texts. Over time, these hymns came to be considered as common repertoire, not attributed to specific musicians or families but shared in the public domain. This helped to galvanize the community as participants in Christian worship.

In the early twentieth century, Rapanui islanders remained receptive to other musical influences occasionally imported from French Polynesia, and when the first permanent parish priest, Father Sebastian Englert, was finally appointed to Rapa Nui in 1937, a range of church songs with Tahitian words were already incorporated into "traditional" Rapanui performance practices. The secular music of early twentieth-century Rapa Nui incorporated fragments from Tahitian hymns and vernacular songs as well, though few of these were preserved in their entirety. Rather, the Rapanui adapted these tunes to their own performances alongside other European, South American, and

Polynesian song fragments that reached the island in the first half of the twentieth century.

Angata the Prophetess

Another turning point in the early history of the Church on Rapa Nui concerns the story of catechist María Angata Veri Tahi 'a Pengo Hare Koho, known as Angata, who in 1914 became the leader of a revolt against the island's administrative authorities. Life was hard for the Rapanui in the 1910s. The island was lacking in resources, and all of the able adult population labored for a sheep farm subsidiary of the Williamson-Balfour Company, The Compañía Explotadora de Isla de Pascua (or CEDIP), that acted as the island's de facto administration in the early twentieth century. One Sunday in 1914 (during Katherine Routledge's fieldwork), Angata addressed the Rapanui congregation in a church service, describing a dream in which God had assured her that it was his will that the hungry Rapanui should set forth and slaughter a large quantity of livestock belonging to CEDIP. As Routledge (1998 [1919]): observed:

> On June 30th, while we were still at the Manager's [residence] a curious development began which turned the history of the next five weeks into a Gilbertian opera – a play, however, with an undercurrent of reality which made the time the most anxious in the story of the Expedition. On that date a semi-crippled old woman, named Angata . . . came up to the Manager's house . . . and informed him that she had had a dream from God, according to which M. Merlet, the chairman of the Company, was "no more," and the island belonged to the Kanakas, who were to take the cattle and have a feast the following day. (141–42)

This incident was followed up with a letter from the community to company director Percy Edmunds, detailing the intent to assume possession of the island and livestock (Routledge 1998 [1919]: 142) and the subsequent slaughter of a large number of animals. Routledge described smoke from cooking fires rising from all over the village, and a new dream-message from Angata, claiming that God was "very pleased that the Kanakas had eaten the meat and that they were to eat some more" (143). News of the rebellion reached Chile, and a navy supply ship carrying military authorities intent on curtailing any further unrest was soon dispatched. Meanwhile, Angata took up residence within the church and continued to lead the congregation in songs, prayers, and dances.

Angata's rebellion was quickly subdued by the military. She was arrested, detained, and prohibited from further preaching in the church. However, some concessions were made regarding the relationship between the islanders and CEDIP, with clearer and less exploitative rules put in place for the conditions of labor. The whole episode was chronicled in the song *O'omo o Niko*, directed at Nicholas Pakarati, in which the final stanza refers to Angata as the *nua* ("mother") thrown down on her fragile knees when the navy "marines" arrived.

WEDDINGS AND RELATED CELEBRATIONS

By the turn of the twentieth century, the Hangaroa parish church became the primary site for community gatherings and meetings, and the mission at Vaihu had been disbanded. Pakarati continued as the Church's informal representative until his death in 1927, assisted by occasional visits of priests and bishops from Chile and Tahiti. A crucial function of these visits was the ministration of weddings, called *haipoipo*, which had been encouraged by the missionaries of the 1870s to counter what they perceived as the immorality of unmarried relationships in pre-Christian Rapanui society.

As attested by the various types of *riu* relating to engagements and weddings (Abarca 2015), a wedding was an event to be celebrated with song. In the absence of permanent church services, Rapanui couples intent on marrying would often have to wait for the arrival of a priest, ensuring plenty of time for preparation. Many of the *riu* composed between 1910 and 1940 were either intended for a wedding or performed in wedding celebrations. These songs provide an interesting chronicle of other contemporaneous events, as songwriters frequently drew on matters of interest to the community, or stories associated with those getting married or their families, to enliven wedding celebrations. Even in the 2000s, Kiko Pate was able to remember a large number of *haipoipo* songs, together with the names of the couples for whom they had been written.

Another unique performance practice, called *miro oʻone* (or "earth boat") dances also arose alongside the expansion of wedding celebrations in the early twentieth century. While not specifically a religious performance, these structures required extensive preparation and were therefore usually assembled only for a major event, like a wedding. Some *miro oʻone* were earth mounds in the shape of a canoe, within which performers would sit and perform rowing motions while singing (Mètraux 1940: 350–51). Others involved the construction of pantomime boats from lengths of cloth or other scrap materials.

DISEASE AND DISTANCE

Leprosy emerged on Rapa Nui in the 1880s, where it became a public health concern of the Church and the Chilean state. For some time, the presence of this disease was used as a pretext to prohibit all Rapanui from off-island travel. Those found to be infected were required to live separately from the Hangaroa community in a sanatorium just outside the township, which was built by missionaries in 1916. During the 1920s and 1930s, this facility was managed by Sacred Heart missionaries and serviced by the relatives of those living within. The sole purpose of the sanatorium was to prevent the spread of the disease throughout the community, as there was at that time no knowledge of a cure and little hope for intensive medical attention in such a remote outpost.

The sanatorium residents were encouraged to carve small wooden statues for trade (some of them had been excellent carvers), and the missionaries instituted music as a core activity, which was more inclusive of those who were unable to participate in other physical activities. Otherwise, the sick had little to do while they wasted away, in some cases for many years. Their circumstances were dire, but there was an unintended benefit to bringing a subset of the Rapanui community together in this way. While other able-bodied Rapanui were kept busy laboring for CEDIP, the sanatorium community had extensive free time to devote to teaching and learning legends, poems, chants, and songs and quickly became a key repository for ancestral cultural knowledge.

An example of this concerns the production of the "Manuscript E" compiled by ethnologist Thomas Barthel in the mid-twentieth century and published as an appendix to his 1978 book. This text, originally committed to paper by Gabriel Veriveri in the 1930s, contained the knowledge of ancestor figure Pua Ara Hoa, comprising a collection of foundation stories, poems, genealogies, and lists of acts associated with the settlement of Rapa Nui and the establishment of the Rapanui royal order (see Barthel 1978: 291–92, 297–98). In the 1930s and 1940s, Kiko Pate was a regular visitor to the sanatorium, tending to family members inside, and he consolidated his music repertoire through his interactions with the sanatorium community. Conditions improved in 1947 with the construction of a new facility, funded by donations from the Chilean Society of Friends of Easter Island, and medical treatment options for leprosy gradually improved. The last of the sanatorium's residents, Papiano Ika, continued to live in a small shack near the now-derelict site until his death in 2008.

MISSIONARY MUSIC AND INSTRUMENTS

Alongside the hymns that were practiced and sung for worship and ceremony, Church ministers made repeated efforts to engage with the Rapanui·community in secular contexts through music. The aforementioned Bienvenido de Estella (1920: 78) distributed harmoniums to the Rapanui community and marveled at the efficacy with which they learned to play them. However, the instruments were probably not completely new to the Rapanui. As Adrienne Kaeppler notes (2001: 48), button accordions (or melodeons) were often present on European sailing ships throughout the Pacific in the mid- to late nineteenth century, and it is possible that instruments like this had been previously encountered by the Rapanui in the latter half of the nineteenth century. It's even more likely that one or two of these instruments were among the possessions of the French, British, and German sailors who coincided on Rapa Nui at the outbreak of World War I. The Rapanui already had their own word to refer to these instruments, calling them *upa upa*, after the "um-pah" sound that the instrument produces when played in a constant in-and-out bellows motion. Some scholars have mistakenly asserted that the *upa upa* was a 1950s introduction to Rapa Nui (Campbell 1971: 49; McLean 1999: 445); however, the instrument clearly had an earlier presence on Rapa Nui, particularly in religious and ritual contexts. Estella's own

FIGURE 2.1. *El upa*. Transcription by Bienvenido de Estella (Estella 1920: n.p.).

transcription of the song *El upa* (Figure 2.1) captured the name of the instrument and its musical motion as well.

There is also evidence of *upa upa* being used in a ritual context at this time. A 1924 photograph from the funeral for Percy Edmunds' infant child shows the *upa upa* fully integrated into the ensemble, arranged in the manner of *huru riu* of old, under the direction of a *hatu* wielding a *rapa* dance paddle (see Figure 2.2). The white linen and floral garland attire of the

FIGURE 2.2. A 1920s funeral. An accordion is present in the 1924 funeral ceremony of Percy Edmunds's infant child. The instrument occupies a central position at the middle of the second seated row. Original photograph provided with permission by Jorge Edmunds.

group suggests that they are likely performing in a religious mode, possibly songs relating to funeral rites. Ever since this time, the *upa upa* has been in some way associated with church music and has been used quite consistently to accompany the church choir in Mass and other church-based music contexts.

German Sacred Heart nuns established and ran a school on Rapa Nui between 1938 and 1956. They are remembered for their use of mandolins to accompany singing sessions and were among the first outsiders to promulgate this guitarlike instrument in a culture that now considers the guitar central to its performance identity. The nuns' musical influence permeated Rapanui popular music to the extent that, in 1958, Chilean musicologist Jorge Urrutia-Blondel captured field recordings of

German folk songs (sung in German, or approximated German) among a range of other songs in the Rapanui language, sung by Rapanui musicians.

REVEREND FATHER SEBASTIAN ENGLERT

The final maturing of the relationship between music and Christianity in early twentieth-century Rapanui culture can be attributed to Rapa Nui's first permanent parish priest, Sebastian Englert, who took up this appointment in 1937 and held it until his death in 1969. Englert's influence over Rapanui cultural and spiritual life was considerable. He was responsible for some of the most detailed ethnographic work concerning precontact Rapanui culture (1964, 1970, 1995, 2002). However, he also took an interventionist approach to Rapanui culture, endorsing some cultural practices and discouraging others.

From the outset, Englert was an advocate for the preservation of Rapanui cultural heritage, and he envisioned a future where the syncretic blend of Christian values and Rapanui tradition would sustain the island as an autonomous Pacific entity within the Chilean nation state, where "as well as being humble sons of Chile, [the Rapanui] do not, by assimilation, lose their unique customs" (Englert 1964: 110). He was, however, selective about exactly which of these customs were consistent with his religious beliefs.

This stance had adverse consequences for the practice of 'ei, for example. The Hangaroa church was well established as the site of Rapanui social gatherings by the time Englert arrived, and this included the occasional performance of 'ei. In some cases, 'ei incorporated gestures suggesting sexual acts, and in other cases, performers illustrated song texts with dramatized physical violence. It was an affront to Englert that these things should be happening in the consecrated grounds of the church.

He prohibited the performance of 'ei in and around the church and discouraged 'ei songs in general. As Englert's devoted assistant, culture bearer Kiko Pate continued this stance throughout his own life, often refusing to discuss his knowledge of 'ei or instruct others in its performance.

Englert established a weekly Mass on Rapa Nui in Latin and began to use both Spanish and Rapanui language in his services during the 1960s. Other attempts at translating Spanish and Tahitian hymn texts into Rapanui language had been made by respected elder and *hatu* Laura Hill (to whom Campbell [1971] attributes some of his collection of *himene* texts) in the 1940s. The Catholic Mass has been preserved on Rapa Nui in this form to the present day, composed of a combination of local and Tahitian-language hymns. Special services are delivered on religious and state holidays, and the Church now offers services entirely in Spanish for the benefit of a growing Chilean resident population.

RAPANUI SACRED SONGS

Anthropologist Grant McCall (1994: 110) once noted that there is only one true Rapanui hymn, *Maria de Rapa Nui*, which is dedicated to the church's statue of St. Mary of Rapa Nui—a majestic wooden carving of Mary depicted in ancient Rapanui fashion with a crown carved in the likeness of a bird petroglyph. The hymn devoted to Maria of Rapa Nui depicts the Holy Spirit "descending" into the carved statue's petroglyph crown such that, when the islanders pray to her, Jesus Christ will listen. The statue occupies pride of place at the front of the Hangaroa church and is taken out in September each year for a procession around the village.

Rapanui sacred repertoire contains a mixture of textual and melodic influences from both Tahitian and Chilean hymns, nuanced with local stylistic influences. Campbell (1971: 568–69) provided a pertinent example of this multilayered hybridity in his transcription of the hymn *No te fanaura o Maria* ("The Birth of Maria"), which has a Tahitian-influenced text set to the tune of *Sobre las olas* ("Over the Waves")—a nineteenth-century waltz of Mexican origin that became popular in Chile (and worldwide) in the early 1900s.

The musical characteristics of Rapanui *himene* do not differ markedly from hymn singing elsewhere, but the performance organization of the Mass is strongly Polynesian in character. Each song in the Rapa Nui Mass is initiated by a choral leader, or *hatu*. The *hatu* is not a formal position in the Church, but successive priests on Rapa Nui have informally supported the role and are aware of its importance in traditional music culture. Occasionally, the task of introducing sung items in the Mass alternates between the *hatu* and the priest. Since the 1960s, two prominent Rapanui leaders have performed the role of *hatu*: Kiko Pate and, more recently, Alberto Hotus.

The *hatu* establishes the tone and tessitura of the hymn by providing a guide to pitch, volume, and articulation. There is no fixed length for this introduction, and choristers generally enter at whatever point they feel most comfortable. Depending on the song, this could occur after only a few notes or once an entire phrase has passed, but the sonic effect produced is a climactic

FIGURE 2.3. *No te fanaura o Maria* (excerpt).

swelling of voices through the first verse of any performance. Given that each singer enters the song at his or her preferred place, the collective voices provide layers of stability, dispelling any sense of tentativeness and resulting in the strident vocalizations marveled at by tourists. Furthermore, the singing is usually homophonic, with parts sung in parallel octaves and improvised harmonies that do not deviate rhythmically from the main melodic line. Triple meter is often used in Rapanui church songs but is largely absent from other Rapanui musics.

The terms that the Rapanui use to describe four voice pitches are likely derived from choral hymn singing practice. These are *re'o arunga* (high voice, or soprano), *re'o vaenga* (middle voice, or alto), *re'o vaenga araro* (lower-middle voice, or tenor), and *re'o araro* (low voice, or bass). These terms align with the relative tessitura of the parts.

While some sections of the Mass are sung unaccompanied, the church has long had a small band of instrumentalists to accompany Sunday services. The instrumentation of this group has varied over the years, but for the last decade or so it has consisted of three to four musicians playing guitar, accordion, and *bombo*, a large side drum associated with Chilean folk music. During the service, both the musicians and the *hatu* sit among the congregation, a few rows back from the front pews on the right-hand side of the church, facing the statue of Maria of Rapa Nui.

The instruments used in the Rapa Nui Mass reflect a history of change through waves of external cultural influence. The portable, resonant Chilean *bombo* replaced ancient stone percussion instruments and the improvised biscuit-tin drums of the early twentieth century, and is played alongside Chilean guitars in church performances. The accordion, however, holds a stronger position in the Sunday Mass, where it is regarded as more traditional. Secular Rapanui performance ensembles of the 1920s and 1930s also adopted white cotton vestments and flower garlands in imitation of Tahitian fashions. Contemporary church performers occasionally use this attire on formal occasions, and they still maintain an instrumental ensemble of accordion together with guitar and percussion. A typical transcription of this accompaniment is provided in Figure 2.4, which presents the first verse of the hymn to Maria Rapa Nui.

THE CHANGING ROLE OF THE CHURCH IN RAPANUI SOCIETY

In the 1970s, one hundred years on from its inception, Catholic Mass remained an important weekly event, as well as an attraction for the tourists who began to arrive at this time. Meanwhile, new social development programs that were being rolled out in Chile, such as the establishment of national endowments for the advancement of indigenous culture, also brought benefits to Rapa Nui. During this period, the church changed from being a site of general Rapanui cultural activity to a place mainly concerned with religious activity. Other aspects of Rapanui cultural practice found venues in government-sponsored programs and commercial tourism initiatives. Therefore, the church became less important as a context for Rapanui cultural heritage in general and more a bastion for the maintenance of its own religious traditions and rituals.

Segments of the Rapanui population began to drift away from regular church attendance in the 1970s, and there are now large sections of the community that do not attend the weekly Mass. Present-day congregations are composed predominantly of community elders, office holders, other prominent persons, and their immediate families. However, much as the ancient Rapanui were fascinated by Eyraud's ritual performances, tourists now flock to the Hangaroa church for Rapa

FIGURE 2.4. *Maria Rapanui* (excerpt).

Nui Mass, and the first Sunday morning of the annual Tapati Rapa Nui festival is reserved for the Tapati Mass, which is advertised within the festival's events schedule. As well as being a living ceremony, the Mass has been thusly inscribed with heritage value. Recently, a new priest dispatched from continental Chile, who was unused to the prevalence of tourism on Rapa

Nui, sought (unsuccessfully) to prohibit tourists from photographing or filming his services, as he felt their presence to be intrusive.

Hymnody has transcended the ritual context to become a facet of secular musical life on Rapa Nui. In Rapanui parlance, the term *himene* is applied to all manner of songs. This includes both introduced songs and a wide range of local compositions. Recently composed songs of any type are distinguished from older *himene* by the term *himene api*, or "new" *himene*. The Tapati Rapa Nui festival includes a song competition category for *himene api* in which young performers are particularly encouraged to participate. Not only does this provide a forum for new and emerging performers, but also it keeps new songs categorically distinct from other competition categories such as *riu* and *riu tuai*. Meanwhile, sacred songs are called *himene pure*, or "prayer" songs.

The other tangential yet enduring influence of church music on Rapa Nui is that the secularization and popularization of Tahitian-language hymns and hymn tunes in the late nineteenth and early twentieth centuries fostered a degree of receptiveness among the Rapanui to other Tahitian cultural imports. This intensified after the establishment of a commercial airline route between Chile and Tahiti via Rapa Nui in 1973. As such, *himene* provided a further point of engagement for Tahitian popular music, including string band music, throughout the 1960s and 1970s.

The nineteenth century involvement of the Tahitian diocese, especially Bishop Tepano, in Rapanui spiritual affairs laid the groundwork for an enduring relationship between Tahiti and Rapa Nui, which is evidenced everywhere in contemporary popular song. Meanwhile, the Church has maintained a distinctive repertoire of sacred and liturgical songs, drawing on Chilean, Tahitian, and indigenous influences. Through this process, Rapanui *himene* served as a vehicle for the preservation and revitalization of cultural identity. Hymn songs continue to hold meaning for Rapanui performers in both sacred and secular contexts, and they are performed in a manner that conveys a sense of connectedness to place.

3

CHILEAN CULTURE

As a result of the affectionate contact between sailors and Pascuans, the latter have learned to know, and then, to love Chile; this is how their patriotism and Chilean-ness developed.

—*A representative of the Chilean navy, explaining the surprise appearance of Rapanui stowaways on a naval vessel arriving in Valparaíso in 1944 (Unattributed 1944)*

RAPA NUI IS UNIQUE IN Polynesia for its status as an annexed territory of a South American nation. Late nineteenth-century Chile, buoyed by success in the War of the Pacific, was in a politically and militarily ascendant phase in the 1880s, and the potential possession of Pacific Island territory, a dominion otherwise enjoyed only by imperial Western powers, was an attractive marker of national prestige. Chilean naval vessels had been sailing out to the vicinity of Rapa Nui since the 1830s (McCall 1994: 64), and Rapa Nui had the potential to be a port for future trans-Pacific shipping routes, as there was no other landfall between Polynesia and the South American coast. Furthermore, Rapa Nui was one of a few Pacific territories yet to be claimed by other imperial powers, so the Chilean annexation of 1888 faced no external opposition.

This chapter relates how the incorporation of Rapa Nui into Chile influenced Rapanui music and culture starting in 1888 and continuing throughout the twentieth century. It examines Rapanui musical responses to Chilean annexation and demonstrates how the Rapanui used music to make sense of their new neocolonial circumstances. It then discusses the key musical influences adopted from Chile, as well as other Latin American music influences that reached Rapa Nui via Chilean popular culture, and explores the ways in which the Rapanui have adapted these influences to advance their own expressive purposes and cultural identity.

THE CHILEAN ANNEXATION OF RAPA NUI

In the late nineteenth-century Pacific, increasingly crowded with colonial and commercial interests, leaders and self-appointed protectors of the Rapanui community began to consider the need for state protection to ensure that incidents like the slave-taking episodes of the 1860s and the opportunism of Dutrou-Bornier in the 1870s were not repeated. The French missionaries who were familiar with Rapa Nui, and who had connections to their counterparts in Valparaíso, wondered whether Chile might be able to offer this protection for Rapa Nui (Englert 1964: 60). Chilean naval captain, Policarpo Toro Hurtado, soon emerged as a strong advocate for Chilean intervention in Rapa Nui.

On the urging of Toro, the Chilean government drafted a document of annexation, which was signed by Rapanui chiefs in 1888. The exact terms of this treaty are a matter of ongoing dispute, and were the subject of a truth commission in 2001 (Comisión verdad histórica y nuevo trato de Isla de Pascua 2001), with the Rapanui insisting that their ancestors interpreted the treaty as applying to all that was "upon the land," not the land itself. However, the Chilean understanding of annexation as an act of territorial incorporation prevailed, and Chile became the sovereign state to which the Rapanui and their island have since belonged.

The Rapanui signatories to Chilean annexation expected improvements in civic and religious services. Such improvements were, however, slow in coming. It soon transpired that Toro had his own plans to establish a sheep ranch there on lands he had quietly acquired from the Church and from the estate of Dutrou-Bornier. However, Toro's venture was unsuccessful, as were other attempts by the Chilean government to establish a settler colony on Rapa Nui. After a few short years, the government handed the operation of the entire island over to a private company, led by Valparaíso entrepreneur Enrique Merlet.

The 1895 contract between Merlet and the Republic of Chile, valid for twenty years, stipulated details such as the number of livestock to be returned at the end of the contract but made no mention of any requirements concerning the island's human population (Unattributed 1895: 531). Merlet became the de facto ruler of the Rapanui, and his business operations produced new hardships (see Castro Flores 2006). Amongst other things, he ordered that the entire population be forcibly removed from their ancestral lands and relocated to a single village, at Hangaroa, to facilitate the operation of his sheep ranch. Anyone wishing to leave the confines of the Hangaroa settlement at this time was only allowed to do so to deal with ranch matters. This act severed many families' connections to the lands of their ancestors, which were later absorbed into a state-run national park where resettlement was forbidden. Hangaroa became the island's population hub and remains the main township on the island today.

In exasperation at the treatment of his people, the then *ariki mau*, Riroroko, boarded a supply vessel for Chile in 1900 in the hope of meeting with Chilean authorities to complain, but he died of poisoning en route. As McCall notes, Merlet and his associates were suspected of his assassination, though no criminal investigation was ever pursued (McCall 1975: 472). Merlet's company then discouraged the selection of a new king, effectively putting an end to the traditional leadership structure.

Having no avenue through which to raise any complaint, Rapanui performers resorted to song, composing a *riu tangi* to vent their frustration. According to McCall, an early version of the song *O tai oranto* (a Rapanui transliteration of the Spanish *O están llorando*, or "Oh they are crying") refers to the death of Riroroko, together with a denial of complaints made by Merlet claiming that the Rapanui population had been stealing his sheep (McCall 1975: 472). Another version of the same song describes Riroroko himself as the "stolen sheep" (or perhaps sacrificial lamb) and incudes a final stanza protesting against Chilean rule (Figure 3.1).

Merlet's interest in Rapa Nui did not endure for long. Having established the ranch's operations, he quickly sought to sell it, and he found a willing buyer in the Williamson-Balfour Company, which administered other business interests in Chile. Williamson-Balfour established a subsidiary, the Compañía

---

Two versions, as transcribed by McCall (1975) and Bendrups (2006):

McCall (1975):

Los Chilenos mentira	The Chilean lie (that)
Los Kanakas se robar el cordero	The Kanakas rob sheep
Oh, 'stai llorando	Oh, all are crying
Finito Rey de Pasquino	The King of Pascua is dead.

Bendrups (2006):

Los chilenos mentira a los kanakas	The Chileans lie to the Kanakas
Se robo el cordero	The sheep has been stolen
O tai oranto	O, they are crying (for)
Fini rei a te pakuina	The end of the Pascuan king
La tierra no pasa a los chilenos	The land will not be given to the Chileans
Hai-ai-ai	[laughter]

FIGURE 3.1. *O tai oranto.* Two versions, as transcribed by McCall (1975) and Bendrups (2006).

Explotadora de Isla de Pascua, or CEDIP (mentioned in the previous chapter), and sent a new manager, Percival Edmunds (who the Rapanui nicknamed "Moni Hiva," or "Foreign Money"), to Rapa Nui in 1904 to oversee operations (Porteous 1981: 45–83).

Edmunds settled well into the island that would be his home for the next two decades. He established good relations with Chilean Church and military officials and with emerging leaders in the Rapanui community, such as Juan Tepano, his lieutenant in CEDIP operations. Edmunds was a welcoming host to European visitors and somehow managed to broker peaceful relations between the English scientists and the German navy and their French prisoners of war, who were all simultaneously present on Rapa Nui at the outbreak of World War I. He was a keen photographer, amassing an important collection of early Rapanui photographs, and he introduced the Rapanui to new musical influences through the importation of an upright piano and a record player. The piano is commemorated in a *haipoipo* song *Ka tangi te piano*, written for the wedding of Elena (Renga) Nahoe and Alberto Ika in 1930. A similar song, in *riu tuai* form, called *Ka tangi te hio a Matu'a* mentions the "sweet sound of father's flute," referring to another introduced instrument.

COMPANY LIFE IN THE 1920s AND 1930s

With a population centrally located around the church at Hangaroa, a schedule of annual visits by Chilean military and supply vessels, and a ranching enterprise demanding the time and attention of all able-bodied Rapanui, a new lifestyle emerged on Rapa Nui with ranching, Church, and Chilean naval influence at its center. Despite the indentured circumstances of the population, some Rapanui welcomed the ranch work, and a new cultural economy emerged around these activities.

Those who worked the shearing sheds at inland Vaitea, for example, considered themselves particularly privileged and captured these sentiments effectively in an 'ei aimed at their counterparts in Hangaroa. Their song *Kanere koe e te mamoe* (Figure 3.2) begins with a boast by the Vaitea workers about the quantity of delicious meat that was available to them. The second verse makes fun of the fact that Hangaroa was where the foreign troops from the *Falcon* (*faracone*) made their home during World War I and casts aspersions on the women of Hangaroa, accusing them of sleeping with the foreign sailors. In the final section, the Vaitea workers assert their superiority by calling themselves "British" (*paratane*) and, in doing so, aligning themselves with CEDIP director Edmunds, before finally boasting about their fine pleated pants.

Other songs from this period pay homage to the military supply ships, the *Baquedano* and the *Araucano*, which made the annual trip to Rapa Nui carrying food, goods, and building supplies, as well as troops. Naval troops had always made a strong impression on the Rapanui, and their uniforms and hats

Kanere koe e te mamoe	How nice you are to eat, my sheep
Mai ka'apa ro mai	And more is left over
Mo te rua po	For tomorrow night
Mo te nene no	We do not eat for hunger
Mo te nene no	We do not eat for hunger
Mo mate mai	But for the flavour
Kahue te farekone	The crew of the Falcon
Ko te nga vi'e	Sleep with the women (in Hangaroa)
Ma rakerake a e ne'ine'i tahi	Making them ugly and dirty
Ka hongohongo ro	Until they smell
Ka pipiro (ro) te nga vi'e	Putrid, all of them
Ma hanahopu korua ana u'i mai	On Saturday, everyone watches us
Ko te paratane o	The British ones
Ka topa ro atu	Who come down (to Hangaroa)
Ku ivi tika a ku titika a te piripo	With pleated pants

FIGURE 3.2. *Kanere koe e te mamoe.*

were very desirable trade items. Early in the twentieth century, in tandem with the development of *miro o'one* performances, the Rapanui invented a dance designed to emulate the movements of sailors' exercises, something they had observed on numerous occasions. This dance, called *tahatirati*, would begin with the shouted command "*forma*" (formation), at which the Rapanui would assemble in line formation. They then had three calls that were given in English, the last of which was a command to "stand direct." The performers wore uniforms that they had obtained through bartering with sailors and mariners, and many of these were of Chilean origin. The dance was still in fashion when Mètraux's expedition arrived on Rapa Nui in the 1930s.

EARLY LATIN AMERICAN MUSICAL INFLUENCES

Rapanui engagement with Chilean music commenced in 1920s when the first gramophone (which the Rapanui called *punipuni*) arrived on Rapa Nui in a consignment of goods for Edmunds. Two others arrived in subsequent years among the possessions of Chilean authorities. Throughout the 1920 and 1930s, these three hand-wound record players were a key source of entertainment for the community. The musical selection reflected what was popular and available in Chile at the time: Viennese waltzes, operatic arias, and early American dance band music, as well as a range of Latin American styles popular in Chile, especially Mexican ballads and *corridos*, and Argentine tango (González and Rolle 2005: 425). Recordings that reached Rapa Nui were played over and over until the discs were completely worn out. The frequent repetition of a small selection of records ensured that the musical elements they contained became embedded in rather particular ways in local practice, and nowhere more curiously than in the case of *tango Rapanui*.

TANGO RAPANUI

The tango craze of the 1920s in Chile was an overwhelming phenomenon. In the media, countless examples can be found of exasperated commentators decrying the rise of this thoroughly foreign (and, according to its detractors, morally questionable) import, which was popular across all strata of Chilean society. Tango recordings, both domestic and imported, saturated the commercial music market, and tango dancing, with its close physical contact and erotically suggestive moves, became mainstream entertainment.

The Rapanui also experienced the tango craze, as tango was one of the popular music genres represented in the recordings imported by Edmunds and others. They embraced the dance enthusiastically, but also in quite an idiosyncratic way. The origins of Rapanui tango stem from the arrival of Chilean governor Bagolini and his family, who arrived on Rapa Nui in 1931. Rapanui elder Jorge Edmunds, who was eleven years old at that time, recalled that it was Governor Bagolini's daughter Marita who was the main proponent of tango dancing in the family. According to Edmunds, Marita popularized the dancing of tango on Rapa Nui by offering dance classes to children and organizing community dances around the family's collection of gramophone recordings. These tango dancing sessions were so popular that a local movement continued well after Marita's interventions, with islanders dancing tango with or without musical accompaniment, and gradually developing their own moves in rough imitation of the steps that she had introduced. Many years after the Bagolini family had departed, and long beyond the playable life of the records they had brought, tango was still being danced, with approximated accompaniment on *upa upa* and, as they became more available, guitars. A standardized *tango Rapanui* guitar accompaniment emerged, with a basic rhythm that is utterly unlike anything played by a tango orchestra, but which does preserve the quadratic meter of the dance, as well as the gesture of the *saltito*, the "little jump" that marks each four-beat measure (Figure 3.3).

FIGURE 3.3. Tango Rapanui guitar accompaniment, as recorded by Tararaina in 1973.

Rapanui tango continued throughout the twentieth century, recast as a kind of "traditional" performance when it began to be replaced by other kinds of popular music and dance in the 1960s. It was still observed in the 1990s by documentarian and author Ad Linkels (2000), who described it as follows:

> Tango Rapanui . . . is characterized by relaxed guitar playing rather than intense bandoneon. The melody and rhythm differ greatly from Argentinean tango, but in the dance itself there are postures and movements that clearly resemble the Argentinean form, not least the very fact that it is performed by a couple who hold each other tightly - uncommon in Polynesian dancing. (223)

In the 2000s, Rapanui tango re-emerged as a traditional performance competition category in the Tapati Rapa Nui festival, with young dancers dressed quite formally in Polynesian floral fabrics, demonstrating a standardized choreography of moves and postures that are unlike any other Polynesian dance style (Figure 3.4). The prerecorded music that was (and is) used to accompany these dance competitions is from a 1970s LP recording by an ensemble called Tararaina, who included this short guitar-based *tango Rapanui* track alongside other traditional songs in their debut recording. This guitar performance style is still referred to as "tango" style and is considered to be required knowledge for any accomplished Rapanui guitarist.

CONNECTING WITH CHILE

For fifty years between the 1910s and the 1960s, the Rapanui depended on the lifeline of the annual naval supply ship from Chile. They endured the subjugation of CEDIP, on the one hand, and Chilean military policing on the other, but they were increasingly exposed to the outside world through major political

FIGURE 3.4. Tango Rapanui dancers performing at the 2013 Tapati Rapa Nui festival. Photograph by the author.

events (particularly the two world wars) and the ever-increasing arrivals of foreign research expeditions. Every foreign visit resulted in new information for the Rapanui, allowing them to compare their state of affairs with those of outsiders, and almost every expedition led to demands for some sort of improvement in Rapa Nui's governance. In many cases, these encounters with outsiders were facilitated by music. For example, Norwegian archaeologist (and member of Thor Heyerdahl's 1955 expedition) Arne Skjølsvold was fondly remembered by some Rapanui for bringing along a guitar and tape recorder for entertainment purposes. Meanwhile, from the 1940s onward, a group of influential Chileans formed the Society of Friends of Easter Island, with the express purpose of procuring charity for the Rapanui and advocating on their behalf in mainland Chilean contexts.

These complementary forces inevitably led to new desires and demands among the Rapanui people, who were increasingly aware that they were deprived of many basic rights and opportunities, including freedom of movement. Prior to Chilean annexation, a number of Rapanui had traveled abroad, and one had even enlisted in the Chilean army to fight in the War of the Pacific. However, during the CEDIP period, the Rapanui were permitted to travel only under very special circumstances, a prohibition that remained in place until 1956 (McCall 1975: 472). Young men would occasionally attempt to construct or commandeer small fishing boats and make for Tahiti. One such voyage arrived as planned though many others did not, and the song repertoire of the 1940s contains a number of *riu tangi* devoted to youths lost at sea.

In 1944, a quartet of young Rapanui men tested the rules even further by stowing away on the *Baquedano* as the ship set sail for mainland Chile. Knowing that the ship would not dock again until it reached the port of Valparaíso, they surmised (correctly) that they would only have to elude discovery until the ship was too far along to turn back to Rapa Nui. The four stowaways were incarcerated immediately upon arrival on the continent, but their treatment at the hands of naval authorities in Valparaíso was amicable. The constant rotation of marines through the Rapa Nui outpost had spread an awareness of Rapa Nui through the Chilean navy, and here, suddenly and unexpectedly, four of the islanders were among them. Curiosity overrode protocol, and the islanders were soon released and afforded the status of special guests. As word of the exotic arrivals spread, the young Rapanui men were eventually invited to conduct a radio interview.

Two subsequent events cemented a new perception of Rapa Nui in the imagination of the Valparaíso community. First, the radio host asked if the young men could sing any of their folk songs for the Chilean audience, and they proceeded to sing a variety of popular songs with familiar-sounding melodies but exotic Rapanui lyrics. Chilean interest in Rapanui music has not abated since. This event was subsequently reported in the *La Nación* newspaper, with the headline *"Nativos de la Isla de Pascua siguen de actualidad: cantaron por radio"* ("Easter Island Natives Still Exist: They Sang on Radio"):

> In last Sunday's edition, we published an interesting interview with the Easter Island natives, who after a long trip, arrived in Valparaíso, and are housed in the Silva Palma quarters. These compatriots . . . are the "men of the [hour]" in this city. So much so that yesterday they celebrated a radio appearance where they sang with guitar and related some interesting stories about their nautical adventure. (Unattributed 1944)

Second, and perhaps more significantly, when asked why they had hidden on the *Baquedano*, the young men answered that, as proud and patriotic subjects, they merely wanted to know Chile, the country that had colonized them more than fifty years before but which very few islanders had ever seen with their own eyes. This on-air expression of patriotism stirred a wave of public interest in the plight of the Rapanui people. The governance of Rapa Nui, which had until then been regarded exclusively as a military matter, soon became a public issue. The islanders would no longer be viewed as exotic oddities but proud compatriots. They had, after all, expressed themselves well in Spanish on the radio and had quickly established excellent rapport with everyone they encountered.

Manuel Banderas, a former minister of education, was subsequently sent to Rapa Nui as an emissary of the Chilean government to report on living conditions there, whence he provided the following commentary:

> Easter is a prison for the Pascuans; the natives live under the protection of a group of functionaries who prohibit them from

even entering the wharf area. On top of this, they beat our poor compatriots, I've seen it with my own eyes. . . . Like some sort of patronizing sarcasm . . . the island is rented out to the famous Exploitative Company. . . . [W]e should be more humane with the Pascuan population, who are living the final dregs of their millennial history. . . . [T]he nation should proceed with immediate colonization of Easter Island. (Unattributed 1944)

In the 1950s, things began to change. Chile refused to renew the CEDIP lease over Rapa Nui in 1953, and the island's governance became the responsibility of the Chilean navy. By the late 1950s, the Society of Friends of Easter Island had managed to establish a program of study scholarships for Rapanui youth to study in Chile, providing unprecedented opportunities for travel.

In 1964, a group of Rapanui who had benefited from these scholarships gathered to compose a letter of complaint to Chilean president Eduardo Frei, decrying the dictatorial behavior of the island's naval governors:

With all due respect, most excellent president of Chile, we wish to express that we too know our rights and obligations, which are equal and the same for all Chileans. But we cannot speak freely here because we live under threat. . . . [T]hey [the navy] inflict tyranny upon us. (Comisión verdad histórica y nuevo trato de Isla de Pascua 2001: 18)

This attempt at communication reflected a period of social unrest, culminating in the community staging an election of an independent indigenous mayor, a Chilean-educated teacher who would soon become the standard bearer for this emergent self-determination movement.

This protest against Chilean naval governance was assisted by the coincidental presence of the Canadian Medical Expedition to Easter Island on Rapa Nui at the time, as the islanders were able to slip their protest letter past the naval authorities by sending it on the Canadians' own ship. When naval governor Jorge Portilla subsequently sought to detain the leader of the rebellion, his police were obstructed by a large group of women who had gathered to prevent the arrest (Porteous 1981: 70–72). After some tense negotiations, Chilean authorities conceded to the election of a local mayor to represent Rapa Nui in the provincial political system. Shortly thereafter, in March 1966, by an act of parliament, the Rapanui were recognized for the first time as Chilean citizens, with equal rights under national law.

Chilean musical influences emerged in Rapanui responses to the events of 1964 to 1966 and the lead-up to the 1970 presidential election, in which the Rapanui were able to vote. The rebellion and the elections provided contexts for commemorative musical compositions, ranging from Antonio Tepano's short recounting of the 1964 revolt *En ese tiempo* ("in those times", Figure 3.5), to political party campaign songs for the 1970 election (Figure 3.6). Interestingly, some of these songs had Spanish lyrics, and in the case of *En ese tiempo*, the guitar accompaniment is reminiscent of the *corrido* songs that were popular in Chile in the early twentieth century.

That musicians such as Antonio Tepano and Kiko Pate were willing to utilize Spanish lyrics suggests a positive attitude toward Chile at this time. Like the stowaways' radio proclamations, these songs suggest a willingness among the Rapanui to embrace contact with Chile, particularly after the promulgation

En ese tiempo	At that time
Ninguna mujer durmió	No woman slept
Defendiendo nuestros hijos	Defending our sons
Y su tierra que nació	And the land (where they were) born
Ahora estamos contento	Now we are happy
Con nuestro gobernador	With our governor
Viva Alfonso, viva Alesandri	Long live Alfonso, long live Alesandri
Viva Pascua de mi amor	Long live Pascua, my love

FIGURE 3.5. *En ese tiempo.*

Ueha ieha reka nei	Hooray, hurrah, let us celebrate
O te paratio	The (political) party, so
Alessandri volvera	Alessandri will return
Viva Alessandri	Long live Alessandri
Paratio nei ko te ve'ave'a	This is the 'hot' party
Ka tutu te ori	So let us dance
Ki te o tea	Until morning
Matou mo rusia atu	We will fight
Ite paratio	For the party
E rangaranga tahi ro	Until all the opposition end up
Te eve arunga	Farting in the air

FIGURE 3.6. *Ueha ieha reka nei.* An election song composed by Kiko Pate, 1966.

of the colloquially termed *ley pascua* (Easter Island law) 16.441, which conferred citizenship to the Rapanui.

THE FOLKLORIZATION OF RAPANUI MUSIC

The gradually increasing accessibility of Rapa Nui to outsiders in the 1940s coincided with the emergence and consolidation of a cultural heritage movement in Chile, in which previously disparate and unconnected cultural practices of indigenous and settler societies were brought together under the umbrella of national folklore. Inspired by the folk movements of late nineteenth-century Europe, Chile was among the first countries in the Americas to establish a folklore movement, in 1909, spearheaded by German émigrés. By the 1930s, several important studies of Chilean folk cultures had been produced, all of which served to support a cultural projection of Chile as a unified, culturally coherent nation state with codified art and performance practices that could be learned and reproduced. A formal Asociación Nacional del Folklore de Chile (National Association of Chilean Folklore) was established in 1943, together with an Institute of Folklore Studies at the National University of Chile.

As Manuel Dannemann (2007: 17–20) notes, this movement developed a set of professional practices for the work of the "folklorist," which included methods for recording, transcribing, learning, performing, and teaching the diverse musical traditions of Chile. Governments of all political leanings supported the folklore movement throughout the twentieth century, with some song and dance collectors (such as Margot Loyola and Gabriela Pizarro) becoming household names in Chile. The nationalistic, completist tendencies of the folklore movement fostered wider public interest in the cultural practices of indigenous groups throughout Chile. This interest extended to Chile's little-known Pacific island territory.

THE FIFTIETH ANNIVERSARY OF CHILEAN ANNEXATION

A seminal moment in the development of a Rapanui folklore repertoire occurred in 1938, the fiftieth anniversary of Chilean annexation. The newly appointed governor to Rapa Nui, Dr. Alvaro Tejeda Lawrence, decided that the anniversary should be celebrated with a concert of Rapanui "folk" music, to coincide with Chilean Independence Day (on September 18). Tejeda asked the islanders to present the "oldest songs that they knew" for this concert and released performers from CEDIP work to prepare and rehearse their material.

The idea of preparing ancient songs for a political anniversary was probably a perplexing request for these musicians, as many of their most ancient songs were connected to specific social functions, with lyrics and references that would simply sound out of place in a staged concert. After some deliberation, they decided that a kind of song contest, or *koro hakaopo*, might be suited to the event, and that it should also take the form of a *koro paina* in honor of Tejeda, who had commissioned the performance (see Campbell 1971: 411). Kiko Pate, who was then eleven years old, remembers a time of frantic activity:

> What Doctor Tejeda asked was difficult. The performers were not used to this sort of thing. How could songs be performed out of context? There were no songs that were just for show, so they spent a long time trying to decide what songs to sing. . . . [T]hey composed many new songs. (Pate 2002)

The performers decided on a theme for the performance, drawing on songs and stories relating to Hotu Matu'a and the settlement story of Rapanui. These stories were both well known and very old, which, they thought, would satisfy Governor Tejeda. The resultant repertoire for the celebration included songs in a variety of performance styles, ranging from *riu tuai* to waltz, even though the thematic material was largely drawn from ancient legends (*a'amu tuai*). The rehearsal process resulted in a flurry of collaboration between musicians, who reworked, modified, and created new songs for the occasion. In some cases, this may have been because only fragments of some songs could be remembered. In other cases, there were episodes in legends recounted at that time that did not have existing *riu* relating to them, so new songs were required. Entire songs were drawn from existing family repertoires where possible, and other *riu* fragments were worked into new compositions for the purposes of the celebration. The *riu Ka tere te vaka* is a good example of this reworking, as the version produced for the 1938 performance contains fragments from two distinct *patautau* texts. Additionally, some new songs relating to *kai kāi* recitations were also composed for the event (Campbell 1971: 444). What resulted was the consolidation of a repertoire of around thirty songs relating to the legendary voyage of Hotu

Matuʻa and the founding of Rapa Nui (listed in full in Bendrups 2006a: 389–99).

Tejeda was invited to play the part of Hotu Matuʻa in the concert, and his wife was honored with the role of Avareipua. The performers were divided into two competing groups (those who lived in Hangaroa and those from neighboring Moeroa) for the *koro hakaopo*, and a concert stage was marked out at the ceremonial site of Tahai, where the Hangaroa group sat singing while waiting for the arrival of the Moeroa group. As an opening to the concert, the Moeroa group arrived on foot at nightfall with "Avareipua" (Mrs. Tejeda) hoisted aloft by the dancers, who sang and chanted the song shown in Figure 3.7 as they approached.

This was followed by alternating songs from the Hangaroa and Moeroa groups, with a highlight being the performance of a new *riu I hea Hotu Matuʻa e hura nei* ("where might Hotu Matuʻa and his legacy be found?"), which is now regarded as the unofficial Rapa Nui anthem. This song has since been used in an official capacity in overseas concerts (such as the 1976 Festival of Pacific Arts in New Zealand) and has become a feature of many public events, including formal civic ceremonies on Rapa Nui. Kiko Pate attributed partial responsibility for this composition to his aunt Maria Luisa Pate, who may have based

E tere tere ana i toʻona ao	Showing the symbol of her reign
He rango te ariki ko Avareipua	The queen Avareipua
Ki runga ki te ahu	Upon the *ahu* (of Tahai)
Mo haka tere tere i toʻona ao	To show the symbol of her reign
He hoko te ariki ko Avareipua	The queen Avareipua dances
He maʻu ite au i toʻona rima	With her *au* in her hand
Ka tau te rei miro tau aro te ariki	Hang the *rei miro* on the queens chest
Mo haka tikea i toʻona ao	To show her power

FIGURE 3.7. *E tere tere ana ito ona au.* Song performed by the Moeroa ensemble in 1938.

the melody, or part of it, on one of her favorite recordings—a Viennese waltz from Percy Edmunds's record collection. Despite the unusual (for Rapanui music) ternary meter of the song and the undeniably Western harmonic structure that underpins the melody, *I hea Hotu Matu'a e hura nei* is now considered one of the most culturally important songs in collective Rapanui repertoire (Figure 3.8).

Alvaro Tejeda returned to Chile in 1940, together with prominent Rapanui performer Ricardo Hito as a cultural emissary. Their departure was marked with another community-wide celebration. On this occasion, Ricardo Hito arranged for two groups of performers to be dressed in traditional *hami* loincloths, which had not been worn since the missionary period (Campbell 1971: 290). Tejeda himself was adorned with

I hea Hotu Matu'a e hura nei	Where is Hotu Matu'a now?
I Te Pito o te Henua e hura nei	In Te Pito o te Henua (Rapanui)
I Te Pito o te Henua e hura nei	In Te Pito o te Henua, he worked
A Haumaka o Hiva	Seen by Haumaka in Hiva
E Ira e Rapa Renga e	Ira and Rapa Renga
Ka kimi te ma'ara o te ariki	Searched for this place for their king
Ko nga kope tu tu'u vai a te ta'anga	Together with those that came before
A Haumaka o Hiva	Haumaka, from Hiva
E Kuihi e Kuara varua e	Kuihi and Kuara (two *aku aku*)
Ka haka o'oa iti iti mai koe	Are the ones singing a little for you
I te re'o o te moa o Ariana	The voice of the cock of Ariana
O'oa e te ariki e	Who sang for the death of the king
I hea Hotu Matu'a i mate ai	Where did Hotu Matu'a die?
I te Reinga Take o i mate ai	He died at Reinga Take
I Hare o Ava o i muraki ai e	And his body was dried at Hare o Ava
I Uraura te Mahina e	In Uraura te Mahina
Ka haka pakako iti iti mai koe	When the cock cried
I te re'o o te moa o Tangi he Tara	The cock of Tangi he Tara
E poki uhi nui o uta ere	The wealthy young man
Oroto Ta'au Renga e	From Oroto Ta'au Renga

FIGURE 3.8. *I hea Hotu Matu'a e hura nei.*

honorific robes: a large *mahute* cape and *hau teke* crown of frigate bird feathers.

CONSOLIDATING RAPANUI FOLKLORE

Throughout the 1940s and 1950s, the songs that had been variously written, revived, or transformed for the 1938 celebrations became the core of an emerging folklore repertoire. When Chilean folklorists, composers, collectors, and cultural historians, including Margot Loyola, Violeta Parra, Jorge Urrutia Blondel, Federico Felbermayer, and Eugenio Pereira Salas, began to turn their attention toward Rapa Nui, this was the repertoire that they all encountered, learned, recorded, transcribed, or analyzed to a greater or lesser extent. The performances, publications, and recordings that they produced made this repertoire accessible to a mainland Chilean audience, and in due course, some of their folkloric performance practices were reabsorbed and recontextualized by the Rapanui themselves.

In 1957, the young Kiko Pate decided to create a new kind of performance ensemble for Rapa Nui, based on Chilean examples. Traditionally, Rapanui performers would form ensembles only when required or commissioned, but Papa Kiko liked the idea of having more regular rehearsals and performances. He had been invited to start teaching music at the island's new primary school (which had opened in 1953), and he figured that an ensemble with weekly rehearsals, emulating the school term, would be a good way to approach this. He drew especially on the songs from the 1938 celebration for this work, as well as other songs handed down to him by his two aunts, who had been prolific songwriters in their own right a generation before. He named the group Hotu Matu'a Avareipua in honor of the island's founding monarchs.

In forming Hotu Matuʻa Avareipua, Kiko also had the opportunity to steer Rapanui performance practice according to his own preferences. A gentle and pious man, he was steadfastly against the performance of ʻei, and was not a strong advocate of vigorous *hoko* or *patautau*. Rather, he loved the melodious music of the church and the melodic character of much Tahitian *himene*, and he sought to impart this aesthetic in his own ensemble. Despite his knowledge of *takona* designs and other traditional ceremonial dress items, Kiko did not use these for his new ensemble, nor did he refer to them in his lessons for the schoolchildren. Rather, he coached his pupils in emulation of the melodious vocal style and formal attire of church choirs found elsewhere in Polynesia. The ensemble helped consolidate the Rapanui folklore repertoire, as the children he taught would themselves go on to perform in and lead other ensembles in future years.

In 2003, the Hotu Matuʻa Avareipua ensemble was briefly reconstituted and commissioned to provide accompaniment for a wedding (Figure 3.9). Kiko adapted the historical figures of Hotu Matuʻa and Avareipua to represent the bride and groom and revived a series of songs from 1938 to underscore their story. One of these songs, *Ka tere te vaka*, was adapted into a modern *hakakio* in honor of the groom, a Chilean businessman, resulting in a song called *Mai hiva Taniera* ("Daniel from Afar").

In tandem with the emergence of a folk song repertoire, the Rapanui performers of the 1950s and 1960s also adapted the musical accompaniment of guitar and *bombo* drum that is typical of Chilean folklore. The Rapanui were familiar with guitars and mandolins, though there were not many of them on the island. However, the study scholarships that were established in the latter half of the 1950s, which enabled many Rapanui to travel to Chile for the first time, gave them access to

FIGURE 3.9. *Conjunto* Hotu Matu'a Avareipua. Revived in 2003 for a wedding performance (Kiko Pate seated in front).

instruments, which they brought home, and increased exposure to Chilean popular music and folklore performers.

This knowledge transformed into new kinds of localized musical practice, as observed by Chilean musicologist Jorge Urrutia Blondel in his 1958 visit to Rapa Nui. In his published fieldwork report, Urrutia Blondel (1958) noted the existence of three kinds of guitar tuning on Rapanui: "Hawaiian" (or "slack key" tuning), *hia hia* (or "Samoan" tuning), and *pascuense* ("Pascuan," or Rapanui) tuning (35). In addition to this, Rapanui guitarists of the 1950s often used the guitar to replicate their vocal line, a technique they called *to'o to'o*.

In 1961, one of Chile's most prominent folklorists, Margot Loyola Palacios, was sponsored by the Chilean government to travel (by military supply ship) to Rapa Nui, in the hope that she would become an effective interlocutor for Rapanui music in the ambit of Chilean folklore. Loyola would later publish a scholarly account of her two-week visit (Loyola 1988). She also obtained excellent field recordings that are now located in the Margot Loyola Archive in Valparaíso.

Later that year, Loyola acted as a sponsor for three Rapanui men who needed to be evacuated to Santiago for medical treatment. Rubén Hito and members of the Pakarati family stayed in Loyola's house for a number of months, where she was able to learn from them, as well as provide the Rapanui with access to guitars and other instruments in her possession. Before the end of the year, she had arranged for them to record a commercial album with her, going by the name "Los Pascuences." This album was a huge success in Chile and led to numerous other recordings for Los Pascuences.

THE RAPANUI *CONJUNTO*

Rubén Hito was particularly inspired by increasing cultural contact with Chile. He had been a key informant in the research of both Margot Loyola and Ramón Campbell, and during his time in Chile, he had gained an awareness of the way in which Chilean folklore ensembles, called *conjuntos folclóricos*, performed. Typically, Chilean *conjuntos* consist of singers and dancers accompanied by a guitar ensemble, *bombo* drums, and, sometimes, other folk instruments particular to cultural or geographic settings. The guitar-centric ensemble format resembled the ubiquitous "string band" format found, with local variations, throughout Polynesia, and Hito decided that the *conjunto* format would be something worth bringing back to Rapa Nui.

Hito also considered himself knowledgeable in Tahitian music, and he established his first *conjunto* in 1963 with the idea of blending Rapanui and Tahitian songs with Chilean-style guitar accompaniment. Rubén's nephew, Antonio Tepano Hito, was recruited as a guitarist for his uncle's new group, an experience he described as follows:

> Uncle Ricardo would tell you to play, and you would have to do it straight away - no checking and no rehearsal. He would expect you to anticipate what he wanted, and would punish those who couldn't. After a while, I became really good at reading him for directions . . . the same way that ancient music ensembles functioned, I guess - drawing direction from the character, the expressions and the body language of the *hatu*. (Antonio Tepano Hito, personal communication, May 20, 2003)

Inspired by his uncle, Antonio Tepano Hito went on to form two other *conjuntos* the next year, Kia Kia and Te Aringa Ora, taking advantage of the presence of the Canadian Medical Expedition to Easter Island, who were a captive audience for the duration of their three-month stay. Tepano Hito had been one of the first Rapanui to benefit from education in continental Chile in the 1950s, and he sought to blend folklore influences with the songs he had learned from his uncle and others. He and his fellow musicians looked to their elders for advice on what to perform. On one occasion, he asked elder Ana Rapahango for advice, and she offered the *patautau E Tu'u e Nave*, which she chanted together with an array of intricate upper body movements (Figure 3.10).

E Tu'u e Nave	Tu'u and Nave
Te huka o te tau'a	Right at the centre of the battle
Ka tahi nei te pua'i oro	This one here, the most powerful
Te ketu a kahu a	Dress yourself for war
Ka ketu tatou	When you arise, all rise
Ki'a hetu'u amo amo	To the stars...
Ki te iri iri vara vara	To the end of the 'Milky Way' constellation
Riu raro riu raro	The lamentable ones remain below
O Vai Nanako O Vai Nanako	At O Vai Nanako
Kere kere topa kere kere topa	As the sun sets
Tu pana re'i a	The shark fin will come (i.e. you will be attacked)

FIGURE 3.10. *E Tu'u e Nave.*

This *patautau* tells the story of an ancient war, and the *hoko* she accompanied it with depicted fight scenes through upper body gestures. Tepano Hito elaborated on these movements, incorporating fighting moves and weapons as props and reinforcing the chant with choreographed foot stomps, body hits, and a more accented vocal delivery. Tepano Hito also adapted *patautau* texts to a guitar accompaniment so that the *conjunto* could use them. These new performance practices inspired subsequent, more theatrical renditions of *hoko* that are now widely performed on Rapa Nui, and which are very popular with tourist and festival audiences.

TAPATI RAPA NUI

In the mid-twentieth century, with contact between Rapa Nui, mainland Chile, and the outside world rapidly increasing, Father Sebastian Englert began pondering whether Rapa Nui might benefit from holding a regular local cultural festival, as was common in many parts of Chile and, indeed, elsewhere in the Pacific (the Fijian Hibiscus Festival, for example, was established in 1956). After 1966, the newly established municipal government of Hangaroa pursued this idea further and turned to a model that was well established in other municipalities around Chile: the *reina de la primavera* (or "Spring Queen") festival. These events, which in Chile date back to around 1915, were a variant of other beauty and talent contests, traditionally organized by student associations throughout the Americas, in which young women were selected as candidates for Spring Queen.

In many Chilean municipalities, these festivals became an opportunity for the performance of local folk songs and dances. On Rapa Nui, the music and dance components of this newly transplanted festival likewise contained local genres. Thus, while the format was Chilean, the content was overwhelmingly

Rapanui. As Angela Tuki and Christian Paoa observed (1991: 30), in addition to providing local entertainment, the festival served as an attraction for the tourists that were arriving on Rapa Nui in increasing numbers after 1968, so there was a natural link between the festival and the new *conjuntos* that had emerged. The *conjunto* soon became the major focus of the Rapa Nui festival, with each contestant expected to have a *conjunto* to support them.

In the Rapa Nui context, the Spring Queen festival resonated with some ancestral practices. For example, it resembled the *koro paina* and *paina tuhi renga* festivals of the precontact era, and its competitive aspect was similar to *koro hakaopo* song contests. The festival also included a street parade (a *farándula*, or "spectacle") of decorated floats showing scenes drawn from *a'amu tuai* or floats with miniature reproductions (in timber or stone) of actual ceremonial sites.

After a lull in the 1960s, the *reina de la primavera* festival format was revived in Chile in 1976 with a nationwide contest, which included the municipality of Hangaroa. The Rapanui candidate, Irene Teave, ended up winning the national competition, cementing the perception of Rapa Nui as a tropical paradise inhabited by remarkable people in the Chilean media. Teave's success in mainland Chile also fostered further investment by the Rapa Nui municipality in the retention and expansion of the festival.

Rapanui musicians of the 1970s relished the challenge of the performance contest, and the development of a *conjunto* competition was seen as a means of ascertaining the prowess of the various musicians who were now exploring this new performance format. One such *conjunto*, called Tararaina, rose to prominence in the 1968 competition and subsequently secured contracts to tour and perform in Chile. Tararaina's leader, Alfredo Tuki, had originally founded the ensemble as something to do with his friends while hanging around after soccer training:

> We would often gather round after football training and play
> the popular new songs that were beginning to appear in the 50s,
> which I developed into a regular activity when I realized that it
> was good for our bonding as a group. (Alfredo Tuki, personal
> communication, April 6, 2003)

Tuki was also motivated by a desire to play something more
modern and upbeat than the choral performances of his uncle
Kiko Pate; hence, Tararaina focused on new repertoire, including
songs introduced from Tahiti, and eschewed *riu tuai, patautau*,
and many *riu tangi* that Tuki and his collaborators felt were too
melancholic. Their open-air rehearsals on the soccer pitch (at the
center of town) attracted many admirers, as well as invitations to
do shows for the island's various expat and tourist cohorts, and
they were eager competitors in the festival competition that year.

In preparation for the festival, Tuki assembled a troupe
consisting of young and energetic dancers, drawing together a
group of twenty-five performers. By coincidence, the Chilean
national airline (Líneas Aéreas Nacionales, or LAN) was about
to commence a campaign advertising a new passenger route
from Santiago to Tahiti via Rapa Nui. The LAN agents who
attended the festival performance saw the commercial potential of an ensemble of young, beautiful islanders playing fast-
paced, exotic-sounding music. They approached Tuki to see if
he would be willing to promote Rapa Nui tourism in LAN of-
fices throughout Chile. Tuki agreed, on the condition that all
twenty-five of the performers were included, with all expenses
covered. Tararaina's Chilean tour was the first opportunity for
many of these young performers to visit Chile, and the first time
that many Chileans would see Rapanui people performing, including songs that had been popularized by Margot Loyola and
Los Pascuences a decade earlier. It also set the precedent for
future ensembles to undertake performance tours, both within
Chile and elsewhere overseas.

Tararaina traveled to mainland Chile in 1971 to perform for socialist president Salvador Allende, and again in 1975, to perform for military dictator president Augusto Pinochet. They also performed in the famous Viña del Mar folkloric festival that year. In 1973 Tararaina recorded a self-titled LP, which sold well in Chile (it was subsequently rereleased three times on cassette and CD). This record presented a wide range of song styles, including references to "traditional" song forms and guitar techniques. Tararaina were also chosen to represent Rapa Nui at a Pacific cultural festival in Auckland in 1973, which was a catalyst for future connections between Rapa Nui and other parts of Polynesia.

Throughout the 1970s and 1980s, the annual Rapa Nui festival expanded to include competitions in a range of other categories, including traditional cultural practices such as hand-line fishing, stone carving, and *mahute* cloth making. The *conjunto* contest was retained as a centerpiece, with bands supported by ever-increasing numbers of dancers (in some cases eighty or more). This was soon accompanied by a dedicated *koro hakaopo* evening in which the *conjuntos* would face off against each other, usually without dancers, in a song contest that would end only when one group made a significant error or repeated a song already performed. Ensembles could also compete for prestige in *riu* competitions, and individual performers could enter contests for *kai kai* (with their *patautau* recitations) and *himene api*. Later additions include categories for *upa upa* performance and Rapanui tango, as well as a *takona* contest in which the contestant would recite the names and significance of the patterns and glyphs painted on their bodies.

The timing of the festival changed throughout the 1970s, eventually moving from spring to summer to accommodate holiday tourism and to enable participation in the festival by the increasing number of young Rapanui who were, by the 1980s, traveling to Chile for their schooling. It also became more explicit in its local focus and by 1980 had been renamed Tapati Rapa Nui, or "Rapa Nui Week" (Hotus et al. 2000: 172). Municipal government documents from this period describe the festival in terms of four key aims: preserving traditions, fostering new artistic expressions, initiating new generations in the traditions of their ancestors, and portraying the richness of Rapanui culture to outsiders (Tuki and Paoa 1991: 30–31).

Since the mid-1990s, Tapati Rapa Nui has consolidated into a permanent summer festival, occurring over two weeks in late January or early February every year. Very little of the Spring Queen origins remain, and all of the competition categories now foreground indigenous ways of doing—from cooking demonstrations using only local ingredients to dressmaking using only traditional materials from the Rapa Nui environment. The festival competitions still revolve around nominated "candidates," but this now includes young men alongside the women.

While the festival consumes considerable municipal government resources, it relies heavily on the volunteerism and private resources of the families who put forward each year's candidates. The family and their formal representatives (*apoderados*) must be able to gather the resources to feed and provide materials for the dozens (or in some cases hundreds) of extended family members, friends, and supporters who undertake the various competitions on behalf of the candidate and sustain them through the rehearsals, costume-making sessions, carving and sculpting, and other preparations in the weeks leading up to the festival. Sometimes a family might begin Tapati Rapa Nui preparations years in advance, to ensure that they are able to support a future candidate.

The private family investment and effort required to enter a Tapati festival is beyond the capacity of some families, while others simply question the value of so much personal wealth going into an event that is ostensibly about cultural identity sustainability but which also plays to the interests of tourists and benefits those involved in the tourism industry. As with many cultural heritage initiatives on Rapa Nui, there is a broad spectrum of opinion in the community about the intrinsic worth of the festival (see Santa Coloma 2006: 150). However, where music is concerned, Tapati Rapa Nui is the most significant community-wide context for some traditional performance practices, such as *koro hakaopo*, and remains important as a space for maintaining, sustaining, and transmitting the performance of *riu, patautau, kai kai*, and *a'amu tuai*, as well as other historically significant genres.

Tapati has also been significant as a staging ground for new performers. This was the case in 1995, where the victorious Tapati *conjunto* became the ensemble Kari Kari, now one of the longest-running and most well-established traditional performance troupes on Rapa Nui. The musicians behind Kari Kari had often played together in the past, and they built a new repertoire on songs they had learned in previous performances with earlier ensembles such as Rapa Iti and Hau Moana. Interestingly, Hau Moana, which disbanded in 1992, had its origins in the activities of a sporting club, much like Tararaina before them. Also, much like the efforts of Kiko Pate in the 1950s, the directors of Kari Kari work with (and mentor) teenage dancers, many of whom are absent from Rapa Nui during the year as they embark on secondary and tertiary education in Chile. Many of these dancers enter the group precisely because they wish to improve their knowledge of Rapanui performance traditions.

RAPANUI FOLKLORE IN CONTEMPORARY CHILE

Since the very first arrivals of Rapanui islanders in mainland Chile, music has been a catalyst for the building of positive, rewarding relationships—as much for the stowaways of the 1940s as for Los Pascuences in the 1960s. The relationship has also been two sided, with Chilean folklorists such as Margot Loyola introducing Rapanui songs into mainstream Chilean folklore repertoires. Chile's most famous poet, Pablo Neruda, wrote a poem about Rapa Nui that was converted into song, and performers associated with Chile's *canto nuevo* folk song movement of the 1970s, such as Antonio Gubbins, wrote songs with Rapanui themes and lyrics (see Bendrups 2016a). The iconic fusion group Los Jaivas staged, filmed, and commercially released a concert on Rapa Nui, performing alongside Rapanui musicians. Meanwhile, the mainland presence of Rapa Nui can be seen in public memorials, including original and replica *moai* statues, as well as the frequent appearance of *moai* and other Rapanui artifacts in commercial branding, souvenir shops, and advertising.

Rapanui musicians are well aware of the hold they can have over the Chilean imaginary and have used this to their advantage in the development of tourist-oriented shows. Kari Kari, for example, have perfected a sort of retrospective, chronological survey of Rapanui music from ancient past to present, starting with some short *patautau* with *hoko* and *riu tuai* and finishing with modern string-band *conjunto* music. The iconic song *sau sau* (discussed in the following chapter) occupies a special place in the sequence of repertoire for the show, as it represents the culmination of internal and external influences. In their early 2000s tourist shows, Kari Kari used to pre-empt their use of *sau sau* in performances with a short but grandiose explanation of the significance of this "traditional" dance and would then build toward a performance climax by inviting audience members to join in dancing with them. In 2003, so many of the young dancers from Kari Kari were studying in Santiago that they decided to assemble their own local version of the ensemble (effectively "Kari Kari Two") in the heart of the Chilean capital.

Another prominent example of Rapanui penetration into mainland Chilean folklore concerns singer-songwriter Emilio "Mito" Manutomatoma, himself a former member of Kari Kari and regular Tapati participant. Mito relocated to Santiago in the late 1990s with the aim of establishing a musical career. While well versed in folkloric performance, he was keen to develop his own songwriting and perceived that this might be more likely to succeed in the considerably larger musical world of the Chilean capital. Between 1998 and 2001, he took whatever work he could find as a freelance vocalist, which involved performing jazz and salsa covers, as well as his original songs, in which he often alternated between Rapanui language and Spanish. Initially, these songs were of little interest to Chilean audiences, as they were musically indistinguishable from other similar pop songs, and as the Rapanui language was often a barrier to comprehension.

In 2002 Mito decided to enter one of his songs, *Voy navegando, navegando* ("I Am Sailing, Sailing") into a song competition that was to be held as part of the Festival del Huaso (or "cowboy" festival) in the small regional town of Olmué. Alongside the more famous song festival of Viña del Mar, Olmué has a high profile within Chilean folklore and attracts participation and media interest from across the country.

Mito was not the first Rapanui to have entered a mainland song festival, and as noted earlier, Chilean folklore was and is inclusive of Rapanui elements. However, he was probably the first to introduce a bilingual Spanish-Rapanui song into this contest. *Voy navegando, navegando* was an exploration of Mito's sense of dual identity—both Rapanui and Chilean. The lyrics conveyed a sense of exposure and vulnerability but also optimism and openness, as he expressed, among other things, a "promise to myself that I would come to know the *conti* [the continent, or Chile] some day." The song was an instant hit with the audience at Olmué and he won the song competition, becoming the first Rapanui person to do so.

The popularity of the song reflected its clever lyrical structure: most of the verses were in Spanish, and so were intelligible to the audience, and most of the Rapanui language sections were simple, short repeated choruses performed at a heightened tempo with a rhythmically expanded accompaniment, making them more exciting. Each chorus was preceded by a shouted "one, two, three, four" count-in in Rapanui, further increasing their excitement. Ultimately, the key message in Mito's song was his desire to get to know Chile better.

Perhaps unknowingly, Mito was tapping into the cultural memory of Chilean-Rapa Nui interactions of the past with this song. Its topic mirrored the comments of the stowaways who had famously reached Valparaíso in 1944. It also closely resembled the prior work of Los Pascuences, whose 1967 album included two songs—*Erua nauka haerepo* ("Walking by the Light of the Stars") and *He oho au ki hiva* ("I'm Traveling to the Unknown Land")—with themes and lyrics that paralleled Mito's own award-winning composition. For the duration of 2002, throughout Chile, Olmué could not be mentioned without reference to Mito. He returned to Rapa Nui for Tapati shortly after the Olmué festival, still on a high from his win, and commenced his 2003 Tapati performance with the statement: "*¡Estamos presente! Estamos más cerca a Chile ahora*" ("We are present! Now we are much closer to Chile").

CHILE, FOLKLORE, AND SUSTAINABILITY

From the act of annexation in 1888 to the promulgation of the *Ley pascua* in 1966, Chile's relationship with Rapanui music and culture was marked by moments of deep engagement interspersed with long periods of disconnection or disinterest. The development of the folklore movement in Chile provided a rational context for this engagement and for positioning Rapanui music as an element of Chilean "national" culture. This contextual positioning endures in contemporary Chile: in education programs, government publications, and other official documents, the Rapanui are uncritically presented as "one of the recognized indigenous groups of Chile" alongside the Aymara, the Mapuche, and other populations. The cultural incongruity of Rapa Nui as the sole Polynesian element in a group of Amerindian cultures with a more or less shared history of conquest and colonization is rarely if ever raised in these discussions.

Where music is concerned, the ubiquity of folklore as a national cultural construct renders such incongruities moot: Rapa Nui is included within Chilean folklore because Rapa Nui is part of Chile. Therefore, a context exists within Chile for Rapanui performances (whether by mainland Chileans or by Rapanui people). One outcome of this enduring relationship is that a space exists for the sustainability of Rapanui performance practices at a national level. This space is not necessarily within the control of Rapanui cultural authorities, but it is available to Rapanui performers who may wish to occupy it and can act as a vehicle for expression of indigenous agency and identity.

4

POLYNESIAN PATHWAYS

In Colour, Features, and Language they bear such affinity to the people of the more Western isles that no one
will doubt that they have the same Origin, it is extraordi-
nary that the same nation should have spread themselves
over all the isles in this Vast Ocean from New Zealand
to this Island which is almost a fourth part of the Globe.
—*Captain James Cook's 1774 description of the Rapanui people*
(Beaglehole 1969: 832–33)

WRITING IN 1774, CAPTAIN JAMES Cook was under no il-
lusion as to the Polynesian heritage of the Rapanui people.
However, subsequent trends in Rapa Nui research have, for one
reason or another, sought other conclusions. This is partly due
to misguided speculation about the prior existence of a superior
civilization responsible for the *moai*, and the misinterpretation
of legends that seemed to support this idea. It is also partly due
to Thor Heyerdahl's persistence in asserting an American origin
for the prehistoric settlement of the Pacific, an idea that has now
been roundly discredited.

As far as the Rapanui are concerned, there is no such confu-
sion. The Rapanui foundation story, as recorded by former head
of the Rapanui council for elders, Alberto Hotus, names several
ancestral figures and island locations that have been remembered in Rapanui oral history and that have become the subjects
of various songs and chants:

King Hotu Matu'a, on the guidance of his counselor Haumaka,
organized the migration effort to reach this land. He sent eight

explorers who encountered the island, according to the instruction of Haumaka, finding there almost all of the points of interest that Haumaka had seen in his dreams. The explorers fulfilled their mission, planting and otherwise preparing the land for the future disembarkation of the royals and their people. Two vessels later arrived, carrying Hotu Matu'a and his sister Ava Rei Pua, reaching the offshore islets of Motu Nui, Motu Iti and Motu Kaokao in the first instance. (Hotus et al. 1988: 24)

Rapanui oral histories and legends provide little insight into the impetus for the migration, but one persistent characteristic in these stories is that they show an awareness of other Polynesian people and places. The original settlers of Rapa Nui arrived on their new island with knowledge of a land left behind, which they called Marae Renga, or Hiva.

Hotu Matu'a chose a landing site on the beach near Anakena as his place of settlement. He then divided the island into two main territories, *Ko tu'u 'aro ko te mata nui* and *Ko tu'u hotu iti ko te mata 'iti o tupahotu* (Hotus et al. 1988: 25), establishing the fundamental territorial division of the island's main clan groups or *mata*, which have endured since that time (van Tilburg 1994: 53). The oral record is silent on any subsequent voyaging attempts, though the Rapanui sustained a liminal awareness of their original Polynesian connections through the maintenance of their foundation legends over numerous generations.

The opportunistic "blackbirding" episodes of the 1860s, so destructive to Rapanui society and culture, also brought the Rapanui back into contact with the Polynesian world from which they had been long separated, and the establishment of the Sacred Heart mission consolidated this connection. In the decades prior to Chilean annexation, the activities of the mission allowed for some limited movement between Rapa Nui and French Polynesia. In the early twentieth century, while unable to travel due to prohibitions imposed by Chilean authorities,

Rapanui islanders maintained an awareness of relatives who had reached Mangareva and Tahiti in the 1870s. Meanwhile, the occasional arrival of Polynesians on vessels docking at Rapa Nui was treated as a cause for celebration.

When the travel ban imposed by Chilean administrators was lifted in 1956, the Rapanui were ready for any opportunity to travel to Tahiti and receptive of anything that might arrive from Tahiti in their direction, usually via the Chilean naval supply ships that periodically continued through to Papeete. The Rapanui interest in all things Polynesian was further stimulated in the 1970s as the Chilean government made various attempts to connect with the Pacific region through a vanguard of Rapanui cultural diplomacy. This chapter explores the musical outcomes of these encounters, providing a window into early Rapanui perspectives on Polynesia and explaining the ways in which this has underpinned contemporary trans-Pacific interactions through music.

THE LOCALIZATION OF TAHITIAN *UTE*

The arrival of Sacred Heart missionaries and their Polynesian assistants on Rapa Nui in the 1860s created (or perhaps renewed) a connection between Rapa Nui and Tahiti and, by extension, other parts of French Polynesia. It is through this connection that the contemporary indigenous name for the island (Rapa Nui) arose. Many Tahitian words were incorporated into everyday Rapanui language, along with terms for different aspects of Rapanui music.

The enthusiastic adoption of *himene pure* in Rapanui music culture reflected local receptiveness to both the religious purpose and Tahitian content of these songs. However, aspects of vernacular Tahitian music were also adopted on Rapa Nui during the 1860s and 1870s. For instance, the Rapanui word *patautau* was likely based on (or modified by) the Tahitian equivalent, *pata'uta'u*, which describes a vigorous, standing dance. Cognate terms also exist elsewhere in Polynesia (McLean 1999: 93–94). Another example of Tahitian influence in Rapanui vernacular performance can be observed in the consolidation of a distinctly Rapanui variant of the song genre known in Tahiti (as well as the Cook Islands and elsewhere in the Pacific) as *ute*.

The exact origin of Rapanui *ute* is unknown. Campbell (1971: 299) proposed the possibility that a precontact performance style with *ute* characteristics existed on Rapa Nui. However, the genre as preserved on Rapa Nui in the 1870s and maintained into the twentieth century differs significantly from other types of extant *riu*. Rapanui *ute* possess distinct and strict musical and melodic characteristics—including multiple vocal parts, drone lines, a distinctive melodic introduction, and a strict rhythmic compass—that more closely resemble Tahitian *ute* than any other Rapanui song genre. Aspects of this particular performance form are noted in nineteenth-century explorers' accounts. For example, Thompson's (1891) description of a Rapanui performance consisting of "three persons seated upon the floor, who accompanied their discordant voices by thumps upon a tom-tom improvised from old cracker boxes" (468) was likely a description of *ute*, as was Geiseler's more generous appraisal from 1882:

> Their singing has three parts with a sounding bass. . . . The principal characteristic of these songs is the deep bass. These songs are sung in a sitting posture with legs bent underneath. They have a leader who gives the pitch. At the beginning of each chant they accord their voices to a sort of scale so that they may appreciate the purity and unison of the voices. (quoted in Mètraux 1940: 357)

These accounts suggest that *ute* performance was prevalent in late nineteenth-century Rapa Nui. The genre was sufficiently valued that dozens of songs composed in *ute* style from the 1910s and 1920s were remembered and transmitted by performers through to the present day. The Tapati Rapa Nui festival includes a competition category of *ute* performance alongside other "traditional" performance forms (*riu, riu tuai,* and *patautau*). However, expert contemporary performers such as Maria Elena Hotus acknowledge the genre's Tahitian origins (Abarca 2015: 209–10).

Ute *Performance*

The formal characteristics of *ute* distinguish it immediately from any other kind of Rapanui music. Like other Polynesian variants of this genre, Rapanui *ute* have multiple, independent vocal parts that operate within strict eight-beat phrases, with a standardized melodic line that is more or less identical in all extant Rapanui examples. The harmonic treatment is mainly homophonic, though the distinct melodic contours move in such a way that they periodically converge and separate, adding an element of polyphony to *ute* performance. While most *riu* contain multiple repeats of phrases and numerous corrective points of melodic reference, *ute* only give the singers a chance to rest briefly (and adjust their singing) at the end of each phrase. In addition, *ute* are usually fast paced, with a syllabic treatment of the text, requiring considerable vocal dexterity. Contemporary Rapanui performers consider *ute* to be a difficult genre to perform well, probably because it is the only Rapanui song style requiring specific harmonies. Thus, *ute* performances are relatively rare.

Rapanui *ute* usually have three distinct voices: an upper melody sung by the *hatu*, one or more parallel octaves, and a low drone line. As a means of coordinating the various vocal lines in Rapanui *ute* performance, *ute* generally begin with an intonation from the *hatu* on the words *e heraru*. While the exact meaning of *e heraru* is unknown, Campbell (1971: 300) observed that this intonation served as a means of tuning the ensemble. A similar optional introduction called *tare* is also found in Tahitian *ute* (McLean 1999: 74). However, in Rapanui *ute* performance, this intonation may then be followed by one or two answering phrases, depending on the number and gender of singers involved.

This intonation and its possible responses provide a wealth of harmonic information (Figure 4.1). The words *e heraru* establish the tonal center of the *ute*, and the first response, on the vocable *e*, introduces and articulates the range of tones that will figure in the subsequent harmonization. The optional additional response, *tere iti*, introduces and reinforces satellite tones above the *hatu*'s initial intonation. By the end of this introduction, all of the vocalists will have arrived in unison or at parallel octaves at the tonal center of the *ute*. Apart from confirming the tonal center, the introduction also gives a sense of breadth to the harmonic texture. Unlike *riu*, where harmonic texture increases during the performance if at all, the impact of *ute* depends on

FIGURE 4.1. *E heraru* and *tere iti*. The intonations for "tuning up" the vocal ensemble for *ute* performance. (a) The first and (optional) second entries. (b) The optional third and fourth entries, if female singers are present.

a harmonic texture being established from the very beginning and then elaborated throughout the verse.

Each phrase of the *ute* is rendered on the basis of a melodic structure that has not changed significantly in over a century. This *ute* melody is repeated twice, followed by a third eight-beat phrase with a melodic line that descends to the tonic toward its end (Figure 4.2). These eight-beat phrases are separated by intonations on the syllable *e*, rendered by the lowest of the vocal lines and often punctuated by open-throated grunts (*ngau*).

In terms of function, there are examples of *ute* that function as *hakakio* and others that function as *'ei* (the song battle between Juan Tepano and Veronica Mahute described in Chapter 1, Figure 1.9, is a case in point). However, *ute* seem to have been used more frequently as a vehicle for commemorative songs, which is consistent with the function of *ute* elsewhere in the Pacific (Alexeyeff 2003: 12; McLean 1999: 31).

FIGURE 4.2. *Ute Ahu Akivi* (excerpt). A typical example of *ute* melody and harmony in the first verse of *Ahu Akivi*.

A good example of *ute* serving a commemorative function concerns the restoration of the ceremonial site known as *ahu* Akivi (described in Abarca [2015: 180] as *ahu* Atiu), or more colloquially as the "seven *moai*," which is a rare example of an inland, seaward-facing *ahu*. This was one of the sites selected for restoration in 1960 by American archaeologist William Mulloy, who believed that restored *ahu* could become a major tourist attraction and future source of income for the Rapanui people. According to Papa Kiko, after the completion of the project, Mulloy sought to commemorate the restored *ahu* in song. Kiko later consulted his aunts Maria Luisa Pate and Margarita Pate, both of whom were considerable musical authorities, about the most appropriate way of doing this, and they suggested the use of *ute* as an appropriate commemorative song form.

The *ute Ahu Akivi* is a powerful song with very direct commemorative references (Figure 4.3). It begins by describing the

Ka tomo ngarepa kepo mai hiva	The young men from far away have come
Ki te avanga ketuketu e	To raise the dead
Haka maroa ite aringa ora	They've raised the memory of our ancestors
Moai ahu akivi e	The *moai* of *ahu* Akivi
Ngakope ha'uru a raro te 'aro	They had slept for a long time below
Karaukarau te ta'u e	For years and years
I tomo te manuhiri ketuketu avanga	These 'continentals' came and rearranged the bones
I haka maroa ai ki runga e	Lifted up and set straight
Ahani ka kore'o te papa'a ai	Fortunately, these foreigners
Tomo mai ai mai hiva e	Who have come from Hiva
I apapa ite paenga i te ma'ea poro	Arranged the large and small stones
Haka titika ai te ahu e	And left the ahu smooth and straight
Haka tu'u ite moai i runga	Erecting the fallen moai
Aringa ora o te tupuna e	The face and memory of our ancestors
Ko ai te ingoa o ranga repa	What are the names of the three young men?
Ko Viri Moroi ko Fikeroa e	They are Billy Mulloy and Figueroa
Viri Moroi ko Fikeroa nei e	Billy Mulloy, Figueroa
E matu'a Sevatiana e	And Father Sebastian

FIGURE 4.3. *Ute Ahu Akivi* (text).

act that had taken place (the "raising of the ancestors") and the manner in which this was undertaken, all the while acknowledging that this "great act" has been achieved by a team of foreign experts. It then directly names and praises the key contributors to the project, enshrining them in the oral record through an act of *hakakio*.

By choosing a song of public declaration and filling it with endorsements of the people who brought the restoration about (namely, William Mulloy, Gonzalo Figueroa, and Father Sebastian Englert), the singers were effectively endorsing the restoration.

THE SAU SAU

In the early twentieth century, following Chilean annexation, the contact that had been renewed between Rapa Nui and Tahiti reduced considerably, and there were long gaps between opportunities for engagement with other Polynesians. Therefore, the chance arrival of a Polynesian crew on board a passing yacht in the 1930s became a memorable occasion for the Rapanui who experienced it, leading to important developments in Rapanui music.

As recounted by Rapanui elders (Campbell 1971: 465), in 1939, a German yacht (*Die Walküre*) arrived at Rapa Nui. It was a vessel with a crew of two Polynesians of uncertain provenance, named Henere and Mape, who were watched intently by the Rapanui on the shoreline as the yacht approached. By the time the yacht reached Hangaroa, the Rapanui had already sent swimmers out to communicate with the crew. That evening, they were instructed to swim ashore where a welcoming party would await them. Meanwhile, other Rapanui with access to stores of food and drink began to prepare a feast for these visitors.

Jorge Edmunds Rapahango, aged nineteen at the time, recalled festivities filled with singing and dancing, as well as much admiration of the guitar the sailors had brought with them. Such instruments were, at this time, difficult to procure on Rapa Nui. Those who were present at this party went to great lengths to memorize the songs and the instrument as accurately as possible, as related by Edmunds Rapahango:

> We had a party at Juan Tuki's place. I was in charge of the alcohol stores then, and I managed to smuggle out some wine for the party. It was like nothing we had ever heard. The guitar was so popular. . . . [T]wo men made an effort to memorize the instrument so that we could try to fashion one for ourselves. Guillermo Teao remembered the shape of the instrument, and Juan Atan memorized the sounds of the strings, so that in the coming months they were able to build their own guitar out of an old paraffin tin and tune it! We had no guitar strings, but these men cleverly unwound a steel cable and used the thin strands for guitar strings, and it worked. (Jorge Edmunds Rapahango, personal communication, February 12, 2002)

By the end of 1939, a number of similar homemade guitars had begun to appear in public performances on Rapa Nui. One elder, Guillermo Teao, became particularly well known for his guitar, which had a body made from an old tin. He named his instrument *pahu peti* (tinned peach), a Rapanui euphemism for "my sweet one." Teao had initially been ridiculed for his efforts, but his guitar functioned well enough. In defiance of his critics, he is known to have sung a song in praise of his *pahu peti*, which has since been passed down in communal repertoire (Figure 4.4.).

At that auspicious gathering, Henere and Mape entertained their Rapanui hosts with songs they had learned in their travels across the Pacific, and there was one particular song,

Ku to'o a te parano	The plans are ready
O te pana pana e	(Assuredly)
Rou rou sevuro e	For the robbery (of vengeance)
Pena oro te me'e o te marino	Are those the 'marines' there?
E haka karo koe	Playing the important ones?
Na kata ro e, e kakata era e	They laugh, they all laugh
I te anga ma'ama'a o te mana	At my crazy work
Na kata aro'e, e kakata era e	They laugh, they all laugh
Kure reva ana o te va'e e	At my crippled feet
Ko te reka ri'ari'a	(But) how great it sounds!
Ta aku kitara nei	The sound of my guitar, now
E riu riu atu ena	I'm singing this song
Ko Pahu Peti nene o te ingoa	For my guitar named sweet Pahu Peti

FIGURE 4.4. *Pahu peti,* as performed by Guillermo Teao in 1939 and related by Kiko Pate.

which they called *sau sau*, that the Rapanui requested again and again, until they had memorized it themselves. It was an odd song for the Rapanui: the lyrics were largely unintelligible, and it is quite possible that it was originally from a language with which Henere and Mape were themselves unfamiliar. They claimed to have learned the song, with an accompanying dance, in Samoa (Campbell 1971: 465; Linkels and Linkels 1999: 95); however, this is uncertain, as the only cognate reference in Samoan music is to an obsolete dance genre called *sao* (Moyle 1990: 51). The exact origin of the *sau sau* therefore remains unknown.

Over the ensuing weeks and months, the song *sau sau* was passed from performer to performer. Undeterred by the unfamiliar lyrics, the Rapanui soon added a second verse in their own language to extend the song. This addition also enabled them to now claim the song as (at least in part) a Rapanui invention. The song's popularity led to entire gatherings being referred to as *sau sau* parties, and this was still the case when Jorge Urrutia Blondel documented this usage of the term *sau sau* in 1958.

Meanwhile, in mainland Chile, eminent folklorist and song collector Margot Loyola came across the *sau sau* in field recordings presented to her by Chilean archaeologist Roberto Montandón on his return from a 1952 field trip to Rapa Nui. When she finally traveled to Rapa Nui herself in 1961, Loyola was ready to be an enthusiastic participant in *sau sau* parties. She subsequently introduced the song into her performances in Chile and internationally.

Sau sau stands out as a unique item in Rapanui repertoire not only because of its popularization in Chile but also because it introduced a new compositional style into Rapanui music (discussed at length in Bendrups 2007b). Unusually for Rapanui songs, *sau sau* contains two distinct sections, performed in a ternary (A-B-A) structure. The "A" section is the original text, with the "B" section then adding the new Rapanui-language lyrics (Figure 4.5).

The original "A" section can be rendered in a more narrow range or, as preferred by Margot Loyola, performed with phrase-end leaps (Figure 4.6). Both versions of this melody are emulated by contemporary performers. Meanwhile, the "B"

Sau sau reva sau reho vari
Erua simo simo simo
Poupou kari, erua makimaki
Mai sapai pahure hia

Ua riro re'e	You belong to me
E mai te ho'e po ava'e	One night, this month
Ava'e haumaru	This tranquil month
Taua mihimihi rea	When we get together
Taua mate aue	We will die of love
A ore to oe riri	Calm yourself now
E Mau Sereti e	Mau Sereti
Ua ho'i fa'a hou taua	We will be back again
Taua mate aue	To die of love
Sau sau reva	Sau sau

FIGURE 4.5. *Sau sau* (text), with an English version of the Spanish translation as provided by both Campbell (1971: 465) and Loyola (1988: 65).

FIGURE 4.6. *Sau sau* (section A). The two common variants of the "A" section of *sau sau*: (a) as frequently performed and (b) as preferred by Loyola.

section of the *sau sau* contains glissandi or wide leaps at phrase endings, and the melody itself has a vocal range well over an octave, far exceeding the range of most traditional Rapanui songs (Figure 4.7).

Margot Loyola made *sau sau* a feature of her own folkloric performances of Rapanui music for many years and, in doing so, caused the song to become hugely popular in continental Chile. The song was recorded many times over, and it was eventually selected for inclusion as one of the various indigenous songs to be taught in the national primary school curriculum. As Loyola herself notes:

> I never set out to promote the Sau Sau. It was simply the most well-liked of my Rapanui recordings, just like it was on the island. It was as if it had a life of its own, and when the public [in Chile]

FIGURE 4.7. *Sau sau* (section B).

adopted it, there was no sense in taking it away. We used it as the basis for many teaching programs about Rapanui culture because it got through to people. (Quoted in Bendrups 2007b: 42)

The choreography for *sau sau* is unfixed, as the Rapanui did not have specific movements to attach to the untranslated first verse, which has come to be performed with quite generic Polynesian dance gestures. This means that Chilean folkloric performers of *sau sau* have been somewhat free to invent their own dance steps according to their own imaginations. For the most part, this ranges from stereotypical "hula" moves approximated from popular media sources to somewhat offensive, racialized portrayals of "tribal" dancing, complete with pouting lips, bulging eyes, and jungle noises. One of the earliest commentators on *sau sau*, Jorge Urrutia Blondel (1958: 21), was critical of the "bizarre exaggerations" that mainland Chilean performers often employed when trying to emulate the dance, but the exotic stereotype persists. This trope is, however, rarely contested by Rapanui performers, especially those involved in folklore dance teaching in mainland Chile, where the exoticism of *sau sau* serves their commercial interests. Ramón Campbell (1988: 14) once commented that the ability to dance *sau sau* was effectively a passport with which islanders could enter continental Chile. The increasing incorporation of pan-Polynesian dance moves in *sau sau* by dance instructors continues to demark it as an exotic (yet familiar) element of Chilean folklore.

TAHITIAN POPULAR MUSIC ON RECORD

Commercial transport between Tahiti and Rapa Nui increased in the 1950s, though it was still difficult for the Rapanui to find funds or a pretext for travel. Rather, the connection primarily served the needs of the island's authorities: Chilean military, Father Sebastian Englert, and a handful of continental Chileans who had taken up residence or married into Rapanui families. According to some elders, during his 1955–56 fieldwork, Thor Heyerdahl once commented that the beautiful beach setting at Anakena would benefit from the importation of coconut palms as decoration. In 1960, Father Sebastian Englert was able to act on this idea, ordering a consignment of two thousand coconuts when the Chilean naval vessel, the Esmeralda, docked at Rapa Nui en route to Papeete on a training exercise. Chilean archaeologist Gonzalo Figueroa was also on board, and his friend

Edmundo Edwards, a Chilean resident on Rapa Nui, asked him to bring back as many new Tahitian LPs as he could.

Edwards owned a radio receiver, but the only station he could pick up with any regularity was an international Swiss shortwave broadcast. Every afternoon, scores of locals would gather at his house to listen to this show, which was bookended with Swiss accordion music (which itself reinforced Rapanui interest in their own *upa upa* playing), but Edwards wanted something new:

> The Pakarati family had one of the old Vitrolas, but most of their records were worn out, and they had even resorted to using a cactus spine for a needle. When we got the new records, a new repertoire of maybe forty-five Tahitian songs developed here within weeks. (Edmundo Edwards, personal communication, August 28, 2012)

Edwards' consignment of Tahitian LPs rapidly changed the listening landscape, introducing a new style of singing and guitar playing and providing new thematic ideas. Many of these songs were derived from a Tahitian dance context, a much faster-paced style of music than the Rapanui had previously practiced. Furthermore, the songs included references to people and places completely unknown on Rapa Nui, but perhaps more familiar in the Tahitian context. One example, *Vahine kapone*, references a Japanese woman, described in the verse as "short and fat, and interested only in money," while another, *O oe te vahine Anami*, casts aspersions against an "annoying" Amami woman "calling out from the street," presumably relating to an interaction on the island of Amami Ōshima. While the origins of these songs is uncertain, the Japanese and Amami references possibly reflect real or imagined cultural encounters through Pacific military rotations during and after World War II.

As with *sau sau*, a number of songs of Tahitian origin from the 1960s subsequently appeared in Loyola's mainland performances and in the repertoire of Los Pascuences. Another song, *Opa opa*, composed by an American visitor to Rapa Nui in 1943, became a standard performance item, as did the Tahitian-inspired songs *Tamure* and *Meriana*, which appear in early Tararaina recordings. The enduring idea of Rapa Nui as a Pacific idyll in Chilean popular culture owes much to the exotic connotations that the Tahitian-inspired popular music and dance of the 1960s were able to impart.

CULTURAL RENAISSANCE: MATA TU'U HOTU ITI

The proliferation of Tahitian popular songs and Tahitian-styled ensembles in 1970s Rapa Nui was conducive to the tropical image that the nascent tourist industry required, and they quickly became the mainstream of Rapanui performance culture, completely replacing *sau sau* parties, tango dancing, and other earlier forms of popular entertainment. However, not all Rapanui were equally engaged in the tourism economy, and some were wary of the cultural impact of foreign popular musics, including those emanating from elsewhere in Polynesia. The emergence of the Spring Queen festival provided the community with a context for performance activities that were intended for local engagement (as well as for the tourist industry), allowing for the creation of competitions in traditional performance genres such as *kai kai* and *ute*, as well as in traditional elements of Rapanui art and craft that might not be of such direct interest to tourists. The expanding size of the *conjunto* groups in the annual festival also required increasing amounts of raw materials for their costumes, and this meant that stocks of *mahute* (paper mulberry), banana palm fibers, *totora* reeds, feathers, shells, and other natural material were needed well in advance of the contest.

In the early 1970s, some Rapanui turned away from the tourist-oriented *conjunto* and folklore performance contexts and instead sought to independently nurture the cultural renaissance that the Spring Queen festival had begun to foster, with a focus on traditional materials and traditional sources for cultural performance. A particular concentration of individuals of the Huke and Tuki family groups spearheaded the use of ancient stories and legends, *a'amu tuai*, as the basis for new dramatic performances, and devised a plan to act them out in the specific locations to which some of these stories pertained (for a detailed description, see Fortin 2009: 60–62).

In 1974, this revivalist movement coalesced into a regular ensemble of performers who took the name Mata Tu'u Hotu Iti (the "tribes of Tu'u and Hotu Iti"). While membership in the group was not intended to be exclusive, Mata Tu'u Hotu Iti evolved as a family-centered ensemble, building on the close relations and associates of founders Carlos and Joel Huke, who shared their vision for bringing "meaning and value to culture" (Huke 1995: 43) at a time of pervasive influence of external popular culture. Mata Tu'u Hotu Iti believed that this vision could be realized through the renewal of traditional songs, dances, and costumes, all encompassed within the theatrical context of *a'amu tuai*, the dramatized "telling" of ancient stories.

In a 1986 interview, Carlos Huke explained that the performance-based cultural revival he envisioned was intended to "elevate, culturally, the spirit of the people . . . by demonstrating the value of past practices" in contrast to unwelcome modern influences (Huke 1995: 45). Leticia Huke, the group's final director, later related that she had been inspired to get involved by the example provided by her own mother, who back in the 1960s sought to revive *tingitingi mahute* (paper bark cloth making) by planting a large crop of *mahute* at a time when practically no one else was cultivating this resource.

The "unwelcome modernizations" referred to by Carlos Huke included *conjunto* performances, as well as much of the performance repertoire of Tararaina and other Tahitian-influenced ensembles. Contrary to the hibiscus-patterned materials that emanated from Tahiti, Mata Tuʻu Hotu Iti made a point of using just traditional dress in performance, which often meant the use a *hami* (loincloth) together with *takona* body painting. They based their performances around the portrayal of entire legends, sometimes including songs that lasted for twenty minutes or more, rather than presenting shorter, popular songs that were more suited to dancing or tourist entertainment.

Since the 1990s, the singular revivalist efforts of Mata Tuʻu Hotu Iti have been taken on at a community-wide level in the context of preparations for the annual Tapati Rapa Nui festival. As Fortin (2009) notes:

> During Tapati in 1999 Mata Tuʻu Hotu Iti made its last performance. The idea of not having theatre during this event prompted the organizers to create a competition in 2000 based on the ancient story-telling practice of *aʻamu tuai*. Each candidate's family had to perform a traditional story or legend of deep testimonial value. These narrations were assessed by the judges who evaluate the fidelity to oral tradition. *Aʻamu tuai* was based and actually performed in the way the troupe Tuʻu Hotu Iti performed it; that is, lighting the stage or part of it with torches, wearing *hami* and speaking in Rapa Nui language. Body painting or *takona* was sometimes used to differentiate characters in a play. (63)

Timed to coincide with the return of school students from Chile for the holidays, families involved in Tapati competitions now spend up to three months preparing for the festival, gathering materials, preparing carvings, rehearsing songs and dances, and doing other cultural activities. This is an important time for the school-age children, many of whom spend their time in Chile conversing mainly in Spanish, to be reimmersed in Rapanui culture and language. Preparations for the festival competitions provide an opportunity for elder Rapanui to pass on many of the traditional skills in performance, carving, and textile production that are otherwise absent from daily life.

A permanent outdoor stage area was built some years ago on the Hangaroa seashore at Hanga Vare Vare (which was, incidentally, the site where Mata Tu'u Hotu Iti gave their first independent performances), bordered by makeshift thatched buildings containing bars and restaurants, called *hare mauku* (grass houses), for the duration of the festival. The stage provides the context for music and dance events, as well as a fashion parade, an *a'amu tuai* storytelling evening, and opening and closing ceremonies. Many of these events present opportunities for the contestants to dress in traditional clothing—often made specifically for the festival—and for the use of *takona* body decorations.

The enduring influence of Mata Tu'u Hotu Iti goes further than Tapati festivals. According to Paloma Huke, more than three hundred young Rapanui were involved in the group's activities from 1974 to 1983 (Huke 1995: 43), and all of them developed a greater appreciation for precontact Rapanui cultural materials and practices as a result. This influence can be seen in the way that subsequent generations of performers have incorporated *takona* and *a'amu tuai* into their performances. It is also observed in the way that Rapanui delegations present themselves in cultural festivals overseas.

CONTEMPORARY PACIFIC FESTIVALS

In early 1970s Chile, the socialist government of Salvador Allende invested widely in cultural promotion. Prominent folklorists such as Margot Loyola were given opportunities to tour throughout the Americas and Europe (including the former

USSR), and various cultural programs were put in place aimed at fostering Chile's cultural diversity. For the Rapanui, this resulted in opportunities to travel and perform elsewhere in the Pacific, commencing in 1972 with a tour to a cultural festival in New Zealand.

The visit to New Zealand would prove formative for the development of Rapanui performance in the 1970s. Elder Alberto Hotus, who was in this delegation, recalled that they were welcomed on the tarmac by a Māori contingent singing a customary *karanga*, or greeting call, which stirred up distant memories for him of Rapanui performance practices that had long passed into disuse:

> We disembarked from the airplane, and they began to sing a *krana* [*karanga*], asking with what intent our king had come to this place. We were stunned to hear our *krana* [*karanga*] being sung by them . . . and we responded in song, because it's our song and we knew it well even though we no longer sang it. (Vargas Santander 1988: 43)

This moment of encounter is just one example of many similar interactions with other Polynesians, in which the Rapanui embarked on a process of cultural rediscovery through exposure to previously unavailable or unknown Polynesian cultural practices. The Rapanui were also very impressed with Māori *haka* and noted its similarity to their own *hoko*. They subsequently adopted certain *haka* stances, postures, and moves that aligned with the thematic content of Rapanui *patautau*.

The Allende government was overthrown by a military coup in 1973, ending many of the cultural programs that Chile had developed, but not the cultural exchanges in the Pacific region. Dictator general Augusto Pinochet was reportedly personally interested in Rapa Nui and its significance as a marker of Chilean naval prowess. Early in his dictatorship, he made a point of visiting Rapa Nui—a symbolic act that was well received by many islanders—and provided substantial support for developing the local infrastructure, especially roads and other civil engineering projects. His military government also maintained the support that Rapanui performers had received under Allende to continue their trans-Pacific cultural exchanges. This resulted in the Rapanui being integrated into the (then) South Pacific Commission's (SPC) Festival of Pacific Arts in 1975—a quadrennial event designed with the intent of fostering Pacific Islanders' cultural identity and mutual awareness. Since that time, the Rapanui have sent a delegation to nearly every subsequent Festival of Pacific Arts, despite being the only Polynesian people to be located outside the geo-political scope of the SPC.

The variety of Rapanui presentations at Festivals of Pacific Arts since 1975 is a point of some interest. Each delegation's aesthetic approach has been influenced quite heavily by the personal preferences of the respective delegation head. In the first few instances, this role was given to Kiko Pate, who encouraged a style of performance that emulated his ensemble Hotu Matuʻa Avareipua. Subsequent delegations took a different approach, leaning toward either tourist-oriented fast-paced *conjunto* ensembles or performances that emulated the efforts of Mata Tuʻu Hotu Iti. On one occasion, a memorable festival performance was provided by a single musician, Kio Teao, who captivated the audience by appearing alone on stage in traditional dress, brandishing two *maʻea poro*, which he slowly began to strike while chanting, softly at first, but then louder. Recent delegations have included whole *huru riu* to sing *riu tuai* and *patautau*, while others have written versions of *aʻamu tuai* for staged festival performances.

The Rapanui delegation to the 2012 Festival of Pacific Arts, in Honiara, was led by Lynn Rapu and featured many of the dancers from his family's ensemble, Kari Kari. The ensemble was well prepared for this festival as it had been heavily involved in

Tapati Rapa Nui earlier in the year, supporting the winning candidate, who also joined the 2012 Festival of Pacific Arts delegation as Tapati "queen." For this festival, Lynn Rapu assembled a delegation that would serve developmental purposes. He fostered inclusion by bringing a broad representation of Rapanui arts, and he included a balance of young and old, male and female participants, such that the festival experience was open to a cohort of younger performers who might not usually have this opportunity. Lynn was keenly aware of the festival as an opportunity to instill cultural pride in the Rapanui youth, and as a chance for young and old islanders to come together socially during their "downtime" at the festival and for further knowledge sharing to occur.

Alongside the Kari Kari dancers and musicians, the delegation included expert carvers and visual artists, such as Tomas Tuki Tepano, who was the recent recipient of a UNESCO art award for his contemporary adaptations of traditional Rapanui carvings (UNESCO 2012). The delegation was also accompanied by the then Rapa Nui mayor, who was invited to participate in all of the festival's formal proceedings. This was significant as it was the first time that an indigenous Rapanui person had received such an invitation. Previously, Rapanui delegations to the Festival of Pacific Arts had always been represented at formal meetings by representatives of the Chilean Ministry of Foreign Affairs.

The multifaceted composition of this Rapa Nui festival delegation enabled cultural exchanges on a number of different levels, including even background tasks associated with festival preparations. For example, the Rapanui carvers had requested large logs for carving (which they worked on over the course of the festival) but still needed to procure tools, chainsaws, and fuel, and relied on local support for this. This meant taking multiple trips out to tool and supply shops with local drivers, where the Rapanui gained insight into some aspects of daily life for their Solomon Islander hosts. The Rapanui festival performances were popular and well attended, as they almost always are at Pacific Arts Festivals, but on this occasion, the festival's theme of "culture in harmony with nature" had particular additional resonances for the Rapanui performers, who had elected to travel with a set of costumes constructed from natural fibers and feathers rather than modern fabrics. As observed previously (Bendrups 2013), on this occasion the Rapanui were:

> Joined by legions of outer-island Solomon Islanders with similar costumes, making them less peculiar and inspiring much Rapanui introspection about trans-Pacific cultural commonalities and shared cultural practices. Indeed, the festival theme, "culture in harmony with nature" became a vector for broad discussions of the ways in which traditional performances use or rely on items drawn from the natural environment. While the Rapanui performers had not come to the festival with much awareness of this theme, their obvious reliance on natural products for their performance culture was a point of thematic coherence. (Bendrups 2013: 169)

Alongside the inspiration generated by performing for (and observing the performances of) other Pacific Islanders, these other interpersonal and philosophical interactions fed back in significant ways into Rapanui social life. Thanks to Lynn Rapu's foresight in 2012, there is now a cohort of young Rapanui who have not only a better understanding of how other Pacific Islanders live but also an emergent sensibility of contemporary Pacific Islander attitudes toward the environment and its role in sustaining Pacific cultures. Arguably, such insight would not be as readily gained from participation in cultural festivals in mainland South America, away from an island and islander context.

PERFORMING THE PACIFIC

As the examples foregrounded in this chapter demonstrate, attempts by Rapanui musicians to construct performative associations elsewhere in Polynesia (and the wider Pacific) have a history that is just as long as the enduring association between Rapa Nui and Chile. Some Rapanui families maintain connections to relatives in Tahiti who emigrated together with the Sacred Heart missionaries in the 1870s, and Tahiti has always been perceived by the Rapanui as an alternative point of cultural reference to the equally distant Chilean capital Santiago. The Tahitian recordings that arrived on Rapa Nui in the 1960s provided concrete evidence of industry and development, and indeed, there are instances of Rapanui singers traveling to Tahiti in the 1970s and 1980s to record their songs, rather than trying to infiltrate the Chilean commercial music scene at that time.

Meanwhile, thanks to the lucrative tourist industry, a whole succession of musical ensembles rich in Polynesian "island" signifiers have emerged and receded on Rapa Nui over the last few decades, with examples including Te Manu, Taina Vaikava, and the eponymously significant Polinesia, led by Pascual Pakarati. Throughout the 1990s, Polinesia performed in their own purpose-built theater-restaurant, Kopakabana (a name that itself evokes Caribbean island references), offering both "Rapanui" and "Polynesian" dancing with explanations in four major European languages. Other groups now offer similar venue-based tourist shows, seeking to capitalize not just on tourists' appetites for cultural experiences, but also on their desire for meals and drinks.

The maintenance of Rapanui connections to the rest of the Pacific serve local needs well in this respect, but they also provide a balancing influence in the island's otherwise quite unequal negotiations with the Chilean state. By asserting their collective Polynesian identity, the Rapanui are able to sustain a level of cultural difference within Chile that would otherwise be very difficult for a singular indigenous community of just a few thousand people. As a Pacific people, the Rapanui have access to autonomous narratives of identity and belonging that compensate for their lack of political autonomy within Chile.

5

COMMERCIAL
CONNECTIONS

Whoever thinks that rap is a modern invention is wrong. This recording shows that many centuries before, the people of Rapa Nui used the rhythmic word, without melody, for the oral transmission of their history and traditions.

—CHILEAN COMPOSER JOAKIN BELLO, *in the liner notes to his recording of Rapanui traditional music (Bello 1995)*

WHEN CHILEAN COMPOSER JOAKIN BELLO visited Rapa Nui in 1994, he was surprised by the strength of the music culture he encountered. Having intended to simply make a few field recordings to weave into his own electro-acoustic compositions, he was captivated by the richness and variety of the repertoire that local singers had at their command. He quickly completed the field recordings needed for his composition project and then devoted his remaining time to recording traditional songs, in collaboration with then council of elders president Alberto Hotus. Hotus assembled a *huru riu* from among the older islanders, and together they availed Bello of their collective repertoire, which he recorded and released as a double CD on his own record label (Bello 1995).

Bello was particularly taken by the rhythmic character of *patautau*, framing it in the liner notes of the CD as a precursor to hip-hop, perhaps in the hope that this would generate some popular interest. This was an unfortunate mischaracterization, but his intentions were well meaning. Just like Estella's description of "ultra Gregorian" Rapanui chants eighty years prior, Bello gives the impression of trying to break through the perception of Rapa Nui as a place devoid of culture. In making this assertion, Bello was, in his own way, advancing the idea that the Rapanui should have a place in the context of a modern, contemporary music environment, one that went beyond the folklore stereotypes in which Rapanui performers were often situated in Chile.

This chapter discusses the place of Rapanui music in relation to global commercial music, with particular attention to the globalized genres that have had a generative influence in Rapanui music making. Some of these have already been represented in the prior chapters, but this chapter extends the discussion with a more specific focus on cultural products emanating from the world beyond the trans-Pacific axis of cultural influence represented by Tahiti, on the one end, and mainland Chile on the other. This includes, particularly, influences brought to Rapa Nui by US military personnel, influences arriving with tourism, and globalized musical influences that have reached Rapa Nui through Chile. It then considers Rapanui engagement with the means of commercial music production, and the local recording industry that has emerged from this. Finally, it offers some key contemporary examples of Rapanui engagement with globalized popular music and music production and describes how contemporary Rapanui ensembles and individuals have been able to deploy these to build their own performance profiles at home, in Chile, and around the world.

MIDCENTURY AMERICAN INFLUENCES

Prior to the 1960s, Rapanui engagement with global popular music was sporadic, guided by the listening tastes of those who had access to records, or by whatever international songs were accessible on the radio. The consignment of Tahitian LPs that arrived in the 1960s was a catalyst for the development of many new songs and performance choices throughout that decade. However, another strong influence would soon follow in the form of rock and roll. Between 1966 and 1970, a contingent of forty-five US Air Force personnel was stationed on Rapa Nui. Alongside their military duties, they assisted in the construction of sewage and drainage lines, provided diesel generators for electricity, and provided a number of jobs for the local community, and their presence was generally welcomed (Novitski 1970). The American troops made a strong impression in Rapanui social life as well, providing access to popular songs that would have otherwise been beyond the knowledge of Rapanui musicians.

On Saturday evenings, they opened their base to the wider population for makeshift disco parties, which became known as "open house"—a term still used by some Rapanui to refer to the 1960s rock and roll music they heard there. These parties occurred outdoors, under the protection of a canopy of small trees, lit up by floodlights and featuring electric record players that could play for hours. The music included, for example, recordings by Creedence Clearwater Revival and John Denver—artists who are remembered fondly by those Rapanui who engaged with the Americans at this time. References to tunes from Creedence or Denver occasionally surface in Rapanui songs composed from the 1970s through the present day (see, for example, Bendrups 2009a: 124).

THE RAPANUI SINGER-SONGWRITER

Where Tahitian songs and Chilean folklore influences both had a direct impact on the development of the Rapanui *conjunto* ensembles, American rock, folk, and country were absorbed in a more individual way by Rapanui musicians who saw these genres as vehicles for personal expression, rather than ensemble performance. One of the most influential exponents of this approach was Sergio "Kio" Teao. Kio was a free diver, spear fisherman, carver, and singer-songwriter of considerable repute. His skills in a range of areas deemed significant to Rapanui cultural heritage made him a much-admired personality. He was a strong advocate for the preservation of traditional music but also interested in the creation of new songs.

Kio's preferred musical aesthetic borrowed from the model provided by American folk and rock singer-songwriters of the 1960s and 1970s. While perfectly capable of leading a group, he excelled when singing alone, with his guitar, and he mostly performed songs that he had written for himself. These songs were characterized by subtle guitar accompaniments and a gentle vocal delivery. Foreign musical influences were also apparent in the way he experimented with chord changes and modulations that contrasted with the nonmodulating tonic-dominant structures of most extant Rapanui songs. He also experimented with meter, writing songs in a lilting ternary when most Rapanui music ancient and modern had a binary pulse.

Kio sang vocal lines that were both soft and high pitched, and he was probably the first Rapanui singer to emulate the falsetto vocal delivery characteristic of some popular Hawaiian performers. For a Rapanui man to sing in a soft, high voice was somewhat contrary to the gendered expectations of Rapanui *himene pure* and *riu tuai*, where parts were organized according to perceived feminine and masculine vocal ranges, yet he managed to do this very effectively, setting an example that other, younger men have since emulated.

Kio Teao wrote dozens of songs, including many love songs. Traditionally, Rapanui "love" songs (*ate manave more*) tended to be written for or about specific individuals; however, Kio rarely named the subjects of his compositions. This made his songs quite popular, as they could be sung in a range of different situations without needing to be changed or reworked. The title song on Teao's studio recording, *Ka Hoko Mai* (1983), is a case in point (Figure 5.1). This song is not directed specifically at a named individual, and it has a verse-chorus structure, with a gently lilting ternary pulse throughout. Kio's voice begins high and pleading before descending into a chorus that is in a more secure vocal range, where he implores an unnamed subject to come to him, to dance over to him.

Throughout the 1980s and 1990s, Kio Teao maintained a constant presence in Rapanui music. He was not overly interested in performing for tourists and so remained somewhat on the periphery of touristic performances, preferring rather to write and sing for himself and his family and friends. He was, however, highly influential in the musical education of his daughter, son-in-law, nieces and nephews, and other young people who lived near his house, which became a magnet for aspiring musicians. He was especially active as a mentor for a generation of young Rapanui men who saw him as a role model: a stoic, self-sufficient Rapanui man more interested in spiritual than material wealth, who was a master carver of timber and stone and a celebrated fisherman, as well as a writer of sensitive poems and songs in their shared ancestral language. Kio's practice of self-accompaniment on guitar was emulated by many of his protégés, who in turn consolidated this style of performance

Ka turu mai	Come down over here
Ka keu mai	Move down over here
Ka teki mai koe ki rote koro	Arrive (at) this party
Ka kati kati tatou	I'm writing for you all
I te riu Rapanui	This Rapanui song
Ka hoko mai, ka hoko mai	Dance over here, dance over here
Ka hoko mai ite taua riu	Dance over to my song

FIGURE 5.1. *Ka hoko mai* (first verse and chorus).

in Rapanui music more broadly, providing the basis for an active contemporary songwriting scene.

Many contemporary Rapanui musicians credit Kio Teao as a formative influence in the development of their musical careers. One of his nephews went on to be the first Rapanui islander to study music education at a tertiary level in Chile. Another nephew, Ito Pakarati, received a scholarship to study music in Los Angeles in 2003 and went on to a performance career in California and Hawaii, where he goes by the name Haumoana.

1970s ROCK AND POP

Throughout the 1970s, Rapa Nui was increasingly exposed to a world beyond the Chile-Tahiti axis. Infrequent but regular commercial flights made it easier than ever for international tourists to reach Rapa Nui, and also for the Rapanui to travel abroad. Meanwhile, radio (and eventually television) broadcasts carried a greater range of internationally circulated music. A culture of appreciation for globalized rock and roll had been established by the presence of the US troops in the decade prior, and in the 1970s, this extended to include a broader palette of heavily amplified hard rock and heavy metal.

An important means of access to this music was the development of cassette technology, which reached Rapa Nui in the late 1970s. Cassette players were portable, battery powered, and considerably more durable than record players. They became the focus of local gatherings and festivities, and owning a cassette player became a mark of social status. A large tape collection represented substantial expenditure, as the cost of one tape imported from Tahiti equated roughly to what an average Rapanui worker might have earned in a month at this time. The ubiquity of personal cassette players in the 1980s meant that tourists often traveled to Rapa Nui with tapes of their own music compilations, which were sometimes left behind as gifts or traded for souvenirs. As in Chile, songs by groups such as AC/DC, Deep Purple (most Rapanui men of a certain age know the riff from *Smoke on the Water*), and Dire Straits were particularly popular on Rapa Nui.

The acoustic guitar was already omnipresent in Rapanui music by the 1960s, but in the 1970s, some Rapanui guitarists began to embrace the model of lead, electric guitar playing that was circulated in hard rock and heavy metal contexts. However, they lacked the instruments with which to replicate this music. On Rapa Nui, the guitar mainly served an accompanying function, and instrumental breaks and solos were not normally included in Rapanui songs. Furthermore, the rock-based music of the 1970s was increasingly more harmonically complex than that of the decade prior and beyond the experience of most contemporary Rapanui guitarists, who were never required to do much more than I-IV-V or tonic-dominant chord sequences for *conjunto* performances.

Determined to find a way to emulate this new wave of international popular music, a musician named Jorge "Zopzy" Pakomio borrowed all the money he could from friends and family so that, when a chance arose to travel to the Chilean mainland in 1973, he had the cash to buy the instruments he needed. That year, he returned to Rapa Nui with the first drum set to reach the island, as well as two electric guitars and a selection of amplifiers. A couple of years later, on a subsequent trip, he added an electronic keyboard and electric bass to these acquisitions.

Zopzy's instruments quickly became a magnet for interactions with other musicians, and by 1974 a band had formed around him, called Rangi Moana. Their first public performances took place in the small bars that had begun to spring up to cater to the growing tourist trade, as well as a recently established discotheque, Toroko. Their repertoire consisted of

blues-based rock covers and their own compositions, sometimes based on traditional songs and song texts. Their amplified instruments provided a whole new layer in the Rapa
Nui soundscape, a world apart from the Tahitian songs and
acoustic *conjunto* performances that the Rapanui audiences
were used to. While guitar techniques were obviously trans-
ferable from acoustic to electric guitar, the members of Rangi
Moana were learning to operate their sound reinforcement on
the go, leading to challenges with feedback, unusual equaliza-
tion, and mixing. However, the musicians incorporated these
effects into their performances. Even decades later Zopzy
was still performing in a way that was receptive to uncon-
ventional electronic effects, making his compositions quite
experimental.

Zopzy approached his amplified and electronic sound
world with the aesthetic outlook of a traditional Rapanui musician and composer. To him, the song lyrics were always pre-
eminent, and all other musical elements played a secondary role
in performance. He used drums, bass, guitar, and keyboard to
create a background to his vocal line, and the electric guitar to
fill in the gaps between each verse, often with short melodic
interjections or just single sustained chords that he would leave
hanging until he was ready to recommence singing. His performances were showy, and he punctuated them with repeated
shouts of "zop-zi," which became his nickname.

In contrast to the tropical prints preferred by the *conjuntos*,
Zopzy performed in black leather boots, tight blue jeans, and
wild hair tied back with a stars-and-stripes bandana, and he
became the rock idol of Rapa Nui. This hard rock imagery endured throughout his life: his final album, *Hakaora Koe – Rapa
Nui In* (Pakomio 2004), has a cover design in which Zopzy is
positioned between two *moai* in profile, with images of his
electric guitars fused to his arms, and with a ghostly cloud of
heavenly light behind him. The album title is rendered in Da

Vinci–style "divine proportion" box lettering that would not look out of place on a Black Sabbath poster.

Zopzy mainly used his keyboard to provide drum and bass loops, and he mastered a performance style in which he would set up these synth beats, add auto-harmonized chords at random, and then sing over the top, sometimes inventing vocal lines on the spot, responding to ideas in his head, interactions with the audience, or observations of the occasion of the performance. In one Tapati showcase, he improvised a song that cheekily made fun of the bands that had been on before him. The indeterminacy of his performances was part of his appeal, but he was a skilled poet in Rapanui language, able to craft witty and cutting lines out of thin air. For this—and his idiosyncratic style—he was a much-loved contributor to Rapanui music.

FILM, TELEVISION, AND SOUND RECORDING

Zopzy's role in introducing amplified and rock band instruments to Rapa Nui was more a product of enthusiasm than mastery. However, his efforts demonstrated that these instruments could be used effectively in a Rapa Nui context, and this inspired a subsequent generation of performers to purposefully incorporate a wider range of rock and pop influences into their music. When commercial recording and performance opportunities started to become more frequent toward the end of the 1990s, Rapanui musicians were ready.

As established in previous chapters, sound recordings had been central to the continuity and development of Rapanui music throughout the twentieth century. From the tango recordings of the 1920s to the Tahitian LPs and American dance parties of the 1960s, many key developments in Rapanui music owe their inception to commercial records. The first Rapanui group to benefit from the record industry, Los Pascuences, directed their recordings at the broader Chilean market, where they were aided by their association with Margot Loyola and her established place within Chilean folklore. In the early 1970s, Ramón Campbell made various attempts to create commercial opportunities for the musicians who had informed his doctoral research, resulting in a number of commercially released recordings. As previously mentioned, the profile generated by their presence in Líneas Aéreas Nacionales (LAN) promotions throughout Chile gave Tararaina a strong commercial position, and their 1973 album was rereleased various times, including on cassette and, later, CD. Their efforts were emulated by other groups, such as Taina Vaikava, who released their own LP in Chile in 1977.

The Rapanui groups who sought commercial exposure in Chile all had similar characteristics. Their repertoire provided an overview of Rapanui music, often including one or two *patautau* chants and one or two *riu tangi* alongside a selection of popular *conjunto* performances, such as one might observe at a tourist show. Invariably, their cover art featured photographs of *moai* or of dancers in traditional dress, or both. All of them were intended for sale in folklore contexts in mainland Chile or as souvenirs for international tourists to Rapa Nui.

Rapanui musicians tended not to take a leading role in the production process for these albums, instead trusting continental friends (such as Loyola or Campbell) or record company producers to determine the look and content of each album. However, the Rapanui attitude toward record production began to change in the 1990s after a succession of interactions with high-profile film and television productions. The first of these was in 1993, when a well-equipped Hollywood production team arrived on Rapa Nui to undertake on-location filming for Kevin Reynolds's blockbuster film *Rapa Nui* (1994), which was based on a mixture of Rapanui legends popularized in the books of Thor Heyerdahl. The production crew remained on the island for a number of months, providing paid work as well as opportunities for astute Rapanui to observe the commercial production process.

The Rapanui were not strangers to film: they had already been the subject of dozens of films throughout the twentieth century. Beginning with Henri Levachery's documentary from the French-Belgian expedition of the 1930s, documentary makers from Thor Heyerdahl and Jacques Cousteau to David Attenborough had produced programs explaining different aspects of Rapanui history and culture. As Max Stanton (2003) once observed, "With the establishment of a scheduled air service in 1967, access to Easter Island became easier and since then approximately two film productions a year have been made there" (116). However, this was the first time that so many Rapanui had such unfettered access to the production process.

The Kevin Reynolds film provided various roles for Rapanui workers in set construction, logistic support, and maintenance, as well as appearing as extras in the film. The Rapanui carefully observed the production crew, as well as the direction, staging, and recording of the actors, and developed an awareness of the inner workings of production processes that they would not otherwise have experienced. It became clear to Rapanui performers that there were many techniques they could adopt from the film set that would enhance their own performance practice. As film extras, they were given direction with regard to costume, makeup, and movement that later served to inform their own staged tourist shows. This translated into sophisticated production knowledge that has served the Rapanui well in their dealings with producers, booking agents, and even sound and lighting engineers in domestic and international venues. The camera-savvy performances of contemporary Rapanui musicians and dancers result in them being regularly singled out for media attention at international festivals such as the Festival of Pacific Arts.

A second important interaction occurred in 1996, when the Chilean National Television Network (TVN) decided to film a soap opera on Rapa Nui titled *Iorana* (the typical Rapanui greeting), which screened throughout Chile in 1998. The show was one in a series of similar productions that had used different iconic places and communities in Chile as the setting for what were otherwise standardized romance dramas in the style of the telenovelas that are widespread in Latin America. Despite the exotic overtones of this project, to their credit, the producers consulted with Rapanui cultural authorities before production, aiming to minimize cultural misrepresentation while also seeking out stories of local significance to be woven here and there into the plot line.

For the mainland Chilean actors and crew involved, the time they spent on location in Rapa Nui was an enlightening experience (recounted in Sierra 2002). Far from the remote backwater that they were expecting, they encountered a community with a sophisticated perspective on film and television production and a keen interest in contributing to the production process. The final episode of the series ended with a voiceover, in Rapanui language, translated into Spanish with on-screen subtitles—"Today, we feel that we have built a bridge of love and friendship across the ocean that separates us"—as a final nod toward the enduring cultural ties between Rapa Nui and mainland Chile.

The production of *Iorana* had implications for Rapanui music as well. In a gesture of cultural inclusion, the producers sought out Rapanui musicians to provide the title track for the series. They traveled to the island to audition potential candidates from a selection of those who were actively performing in tourist shows and recruited a group of young men who were taken back to Santiago to produce the recording. This group included some emerging songwriters (including the previously mentioned Mito Manutomatoma) who performed from time to time with each other and who had a shared knowledge of repertoire, drawn especially from the mentorship of Kio Teao. They rehearsed various options for the soundtrack before deciding on a version of a popular *riu* from the early twentieth century, *E nua e koro* ("Oh Mother, Oh Father").

Their version of this song began with an unaccompanied vocal verse, before adding ukulele, guitar, electric bass, and an overdubbed drum track featuring tom-toms at various pitches. A number of other Rapanui songs were used for the underscore throughout the series, drawn from available commercial sources such as the 1973 Tararaina LP. Another original song by the group that recorded the title track was used to underscore one of the plot lines in the series—a recurring reference to a mysterious female singer who is not revealed until the very final episode, when she is depicted singing on the foreshore.

During the recording in Santiago, the Rapanui musicians developed a rapport with the studio engineers, and toward the end of the process, they negotiated for extra studio time to record some of their other original songs. These became the basis for an album in 1998, for which the group adopted the name Matato'a ("eye of the warrior," an ancient Rapanui term for a rank of fighter or guardian). Manutomatoma stepped away from the project to pursue his own musical trajectory, but the band coalesced under the direction of Keva Atan and embarked on a trajectory that would lead to international recognition on a level not previously experienced by any Rapanui ensemble.

MATATO'A

The album that launched Matato'a was called *Tamai* and subtitled "No to War" in English. It was similar to previous Rapanui productions in its inclusion of older *riu* (like *E nua e koro*) and songs derived from *patautau* texts. However, it also encapsulated a generational shift in terms of the songwriting and musical palette. The album included original songs that commented broadly on contemporary Rapa Nui life. It also featured a number of virtuosic electric guitar lines and riffs and a rock backline arrangement influenced by globalized reggae (see Bendrups 2006b). Reggae was already well established across the Pacific Islands in the 1990s (see Bendrups et al. 2018), but this was the first example of reggae influences appearing in a Rapanui music context.

The title track of the 1998 album, *Tamai*, illustrates both the connections to the past and the new direction being taken by Matato'a (Figure 5.2). Textually, the track is based on segments of the Hetereki *patautau*, transformed into four-bar phrases that suit a popular music context. Matato'a was not the first to do this: fragments of the *patautau* had been repurposed for songs in the fiftieth anniversary concert of 1938, and these songs were subsequently recorded by Tararaina in 1973, including one they called *Kahuira Kahuria*, which was in turn

Verse 1 (*Hetereki patautau*):

Kahuira kahuria te tau'a nei e	Like a lightening bolt, return fighters
E Renga Mitimiti a Vai e	Oh Renga Mitimiti (daughter of) Vai
Mai vara vara tuna	Come, disband
Mai taki taki tuna	Come, disperse
te tangi o te ariki	Cry for (remember) the king

Chorus:

Hotu Matu'a	Hotu Matu'a
Hotu Matu'a	Hotu Matu'a

Verse 2 (*Ka tere te vaka*):

Tere te vake nei hotu Matu'a	Turn the boat of Hotu Matu'a
Mimiro te vaka o Avareipua	Hold the boat of Avareipua

FIGURE 5.2. *Tamai*, as performed by Matato'a, with segments from two separate *patautau* texts as verses.

the basis for the text used by Matato'a in 1998. The song also includes a phrase drawn from the *Ka tere te vaka patautau*, but the Tararaina version didn't draw attention to this. To reconcile the thematic distance between the two texts, Matato'a added a melodic interlude with a phrase that inserted a reference to foundation king Hotu Matu'a into the end of the text borrowed from the *Hetereki patautau*, "*te tangi o te ariki Hotu Matu'a*" (cry for the king Hotu Matu'a), so that the shift to "*ka tere te vaka*" in the following verse would make more sense.

The musical introduction to *Tamai* begins with a soaring electric guitar line that is then joined by back-beat keyboard chords that set up the reggae feel. This is then filled out with an electric bass and drum set track providing a standard rock beat, but one that is heavy in high hat and other cymbals, as well as tom-tom fills based on the overdubs that had been used prominently in the mix for the *Iorana* title track. These production characteristics demonstrate two things: first, the musicians of Matato'a had been paying close attention to the recording process for *Iorana* and had already picked up on useful techniques, and second, they had identified and steered their songs toward a commercial music niche that, while not yet widely performed on Rapa Nui, was ubiquitous in the Pacific and popular around the world.

While not strictly a reggae band, the subtle reggae flavor of their music made Matato'a comparable to other international "world music" productions of the late 1990s and made their music accessible to international markets. However, this was tempered by a desire to remain true to Rapanui culture. A key concern of band leader Keva Atan was that they should strive to always be identifiably Rapanui. They achieved this through clever manipulation of the production process. Many of their studio recordings commenced with a cappella vocals, positioning Rapanui language, and iconic Rapanui melodic forms such as that of *riu tuai* in the forefront of the track. They also often foregrounded amplified ukulele as the "lead" instrument over the top of other instruments, which, while not unique to Rapa Nui, was nevertheless a clear musical signifier of the Pacific.

Following the launch of their first CD, the members of Matato'a found themselves in demand for tourist-oriented performances on Rapa Nui, and they therefore added a dance element to their shows. They engaged a small ensemble of male and female dancers (usually between four and eight performers) who were integrated into "the band," making it more like the *conjunto* ensembles that otherwise inhabited this performance niche. The band also alternated between wearing a uniform of black jeans and T-shirts with bright yellow *takona* prints (designed by Keva) and an outfit of *hami* loincloths and full-body *takona*, sometimes using both costume settings for different sets within a single show for enhanced visual effect.

Matato'a secured a recording deal with EMI Chile for their second CD and soon developed an international touring schedule. They were particularly sought after for festivals across the Pacific, with memorable performances at the Austronesian festival of Taitung (Taiwan) and the Borneo Rainforest Music Festival in the early 2000s. Their engagement with the Borneo Rainforest Music Festival in particular provides an indication of the band's strategic cultural positioning as pan-Pacific artists, as described in a 2002 festival press release:

> Being of Austronesian stock, and at the easternmost extremity of the great Austronesian maritime migrations that for centuries spanned the globe from Madagascar to Easter Island, the Rapa Nui are in fact long lost cousins of the ancestors of the people of Borneo. It will be an amazing meeting of the long separated cultures when Matato'a arrives in Sarawak, where they will be able to recognize some common cultural traits with the cultures of Borneo. (Jun Lin 2002, quoted in Bendrups 2011c: 270)

Such descriptions served the commercial acumen of Matato'a in their engagement with international audiences over the course of a decade, but they also served to remind the performers of their Oceanic heritage, which sets them apart from Chile.

This touring schedule was enabled by the development of a commercial website that enabled international purchases of Matato'a CDs and merchandise, advertised tour dates, and invited new bookings. Between 2003 and 2008, the band was on an almost constant international touring schedule, which included serving as the Rapa Nui delegation to the Festival of Pacific Arts in 2004 and 2008. At the 2008 festival in American Samoa, they headlined alongside other Pacific performers with strong commercial profiles, including King Kapisi and the Fijian band Black Rose. Matato'a was also the first Rapanui band to produce commercial music videos (with Mangrove Studios, in Noumea), including the song *Tamai*, discussed earlier (see Matato'a 2004).

The success of Matato'a had three important implications for Rapanui music in the early twenty-first century. First, they demonstrated that there was a commercial market for Rapanui music, including traditional songs and performance practices, well beyond that of Chilean folklore. Second, they demonstrated that it was possible to make a sustainable living from music. Third, they showed that there was a place for contemporary Rapanui musicians on the world stage. Keva Atan suffered an untimely death in a vehicular accident in 2013, and the band chose not to continue without him. However, some of the musicians and dancers later re-formed into a new ensemble, Mana Tupuna, which continued the performance model of Matato'a but not the touring schedule, instead setting up their own tourist venue in Hangaroa.

MITO AND FUSIÓN RAPA NUI

After his success at the Olmué festival in 2002, Mito Manutomatoma was in strong demand in the Chilean media. He was invited to appear on a variety of television shows, including a guest appearance on TVN's *Tocando las Estrellas* (Touching the Stars) and on *Rojo* (Red) talent quests as a Rapanui dance instructor, and he would later embark on performance tours to Spain and Mexico. In late 2002, he produced a new CD of mostly original material, and on this occasion, the album was marketed in conjunction with a national tour, together with the mainland Chilean studio musicians who contributed to the recording. After a few weeks on the road, Mito suggested that they form a new band called Fusión Rapa Nui in recognition of both the group's cultural mix and its musical style.

Alongside Matato'a, Mito and Fusión Rapa Nui revolutionized the way that Rapanui music was perceived in Chile. First, the band comprised both Rapanui and mainland Chilean members with their own established profiles in different popular music scenes. Second, the idea of "fusion" they were tapping into had a long trajectory in Chilean popular music via the *fusión latinoamericana* movement. Originating in 1960s Santiago, *fusión latinoamericana* was the product of a generation of musicians' attempts to establish an expressive art form that could encompass a broad sense of national cultural identity. These musicians embraced local *folclore*, as well as international popular music (especially rock and jazz), and sought to combine them with musical influences and instruments from Chile's indigenous cultures.

Some *fusión latinoamericana* groups, notably Inti Illimani and Quilapayún, were philosophically aligned with the socialist politics of 1960s Chile, but others were less openly political, gravitating instead toward a spiritually or geographically anchored projection of place and belonging. Prominent 1970s groups such as Los Jaivas and Congreso consolidated *fusión latinoamericana* as a mainstream element of Chilean popular music, with performances that featured Andean aerophones alongside Western wind and brass instruments, as well as indigenous percussion, *charango* and other stringed instruments, and rock-band instrumentation. Their compositions, which were influenced by acid jazz, jazz-rock fusion, and other 1970s genres, were often inspired by or based on iconic, special places in Chile and Latin America.

This preoccupation with place and identity, combined with a musical combination of rock and indigenous elements, was a creatively nurturing and commercially effective platform for Mito and Fusión Rapa Nui in the 2000s. The band was composed of musicians with formal musical training and extensive gigging experience, and Mito provided a unique Rapanui perspective on Chilean identity. Their debut CD, *Mito y Fusión Rapa Nui* (2002), featured a composition by Mito that expresses love and longing for his island home, entitled *Rapa Nui*. Echoing the symbolic and cultural references that appear in many *fusión latinoamericana* works, the chorus of *Rapa Nui* lists key symbols of Rapanui cultural heritage, such as the *rongo rongo* writing system and the island's ancient *manu uru* (wise men), as markers of cultural identity. *Rapa Nui* is rendered complete with strong signifiers of Rapanui music, such as amplified ukulele, the harmonic texture of the accordion, and the use of *bombo*, over quite standard rock-based melodic and harmonic underpinnings.

Mito's association with the domain of *fusión latinoamericana* was also reflected in his collaborations with former Congreso guitarist and composer Joe Vasconcellos. In 2002, Mito and Vasconcellos cowrote the soundtrack for *Ogú y Mampato en Rapa Nui*—an animated film based on a cult Chilean graphic novel series created by Eduardo Armstrong and Themo Lobos (similar in style to the Tin Tin or Asterix graphic novels that are more well known internationally). The film presents a narrative based around the youth Mampato and his caveman companion Ogú, who travel back in time to ancient Rapa Nui. They arrive at Ranu Raraku, where they observe the *moai* quarry in action, and become involved in the *tangata manu* ceremony at Orongo, ultimately assisting in the resolution of an island-wide dispute.

Mito's contribution to the soundtrack for *Ogú y Mampato en Rapa Nui* included elements of traditional *riu, patautau,* and *ute,* as well as his own original songs (see Bendrups 2009b). Vasconcellos and Mito also reworked some of the soundtrack as songs for inclusion on the album *Mito y Fusión Rapa Nui* (2002). The film received international attention because it was the first animated feature film to be produced in South America, and the album went on to win a Chilean music industry award for folklore in 2003.

A LOCAL RECORDING INDUSTRY

The mainland and international success of Matato'a and Mito y Fusión Rapa Nui in the 2000s was keenly observed on Rapa Nui. The size and portability of CDs had made sound recordings viable as souvenir items, for sale to tourists, in the 1990s. Prior to the emergence of Web 2.0 social media platforms, they were also the primary means by which Rapanui musicians might seek to engage with promoters and audiences overseas. However, studio recording required travel to mainland Chile, or at least mixing and mastering in mainland studios, which was time consuming and expensive.

As has been observed elsewhere in the Pacific, computer technology revolutionized the recording industry in the 2000s with the rise of home recording. The increasing availability of inexpensive software and portable hardware brought recording technology to many islands, and it became more economically viable to set up small-scale recording studios in places where distance and hardware costs would have previously been prohibitive. By the early 2000s, this revolution reached Rapa Nui as well.

In conjunction with the production of *Iorana*, Matato'a worked with a mainland Chilean keyboardist who became a member of the group and, in 1999, decided to relocate to Rapa Nui together with his family. His wife was an established Chilean singer and performance artist and relished the opportunity to move to the island, which she believed would be an artistically nurturing space. Shortly after their arrival, she was awarded funding for a major performance work based on Rapanui legends, titled *Nuku te Mango*, which enabled collaborations with Rapanui performers and artists in a range of creative fields. Through her collaborations and his ongoing role in Matato'a, they became aware of widespread enthusiasm for sound recording and, sensing both the need and the opportunity, established a small recording studio, also named Nuku te Mango, on Rapa Nui in 2002.

Nuku te Mango provided Rapanui performers, including many aspiring musicians, with a local space in which to workshop their compositions, and the studio owners worked effectively to broker relationships with potential labels and outlets for this music in continental Chile. From the outset, Nuku te Mango worked with individual artists' creative projects but also sought to actively engage in projects that more directly supported Rapanui cultural heritage, often on a voluntary basis. For example, in 2002, they collaborated with the government-funded indigenous development agency Tarai Henua and the Rapa Nui tourism board to produce a compilation CD of Rapanui music, titled *Mana Tupuna* (Ancestral Power). This was quite an innovative project, as it was the first time that a range of Rapanui musicians, who usually competed with each other for tourist patronage, worked together toward a collaborative production. The completion of this project led to further Chilean government funding, which Tarai Henua used to engage Chilean record producer Claudio Quiñones to come to Rapa Nui to give workshops on copyright and to conduct a scoping study on the potential for Rapanui music to reach more international markets.

Subsequently, Nuku te Mango began commissioning projects in areas of perceived cultural need. For example, in the late 2000s, they collaborated with *kai kai* experts to produce a CD of *kai kai* recitations with an extensively researched booklet that was also a repository of knowledge about this ancient genre. Nuku te Mango also provided recordings to accompany a range of books on different aspects of Rapanui culture published by Rapa Nui Press. The presence of a local recording studio led to a surge in applications by Rapanui for development funding to support recording projects in the 2000s. Meanwhile, some families used the studio as a means for recording the knowledge and experiences of elder family members, for archival purposes rather than commercial ones. The demand for studio time was so strong that, in the latter 2000s, a second recording studio appeared on Rapa Nui, which had a population of only around four thousand people at the time.

By the early 2010s, Nuko te Mango had recorded, mixed, or produced nearly fifty different recording projects and had enough ongoing work commissioned to begin publishing works under their own label. Whether directly intended for tourism or not, what these projects all reveal is a collective desire among Rapanui musicians and families to exert a measure of control over the recording and production process and, in doing so, to assert agency in the manner of their cultural representation. The presence of the studio, combined with the availability of government funding to support recording projects and the willingness of Nuku te Mango to support culturally significant projects, provided the basis for a remarkable legacy of sound recordings.

RAPANUI MUSIC IN THE TWENTY-FIRST CENTURY

In the first decade of the twenty-first century, the combined effects of success in Chile, international exposure, access to recording technologies, and increased collaboration with professional musicians in Chile and elsewhere allowed Rapanui music to move beyond folklore stereotypes and into a new expressive phase. On the one hand, this shift was reflected in the mainstreaming of Rapanui musicians who were no longer expected to just reproduce folkloric shows (see Bendrups 2016a). On the other hand, Rapanui musicians were drawing a wider range of influences into their culturally located performances (including tourist shows) and accepting a broader definition for what might constitute "authentic" cultural expression.

One of the effects of these changes is that contemporary Rapanui musicians had more artistic and commercial freedom than in previous generations, making it possible to develop and sustain professional careers well beyond the Chilean folklore context. The success of Ito Pakarati, who was awarded a scholarship to study music in Los Angeles in 2002 and who has since established a performance niche in Hawaii, is one example of this. Another is that of Yoyo Tuki, who met his Norfolk Islander wife at a Festival of Pacific Arts and emigrated to live with her in Australia, where he has established a performance profile.

Perhaps the most unique example concerns classical pianist Mahani Teave, who was coached from a young age by Chilean virtuoso Roberto Bravo in the 1990s, and then sponsored to study in Europe. Teave developed a command of the concert piano repertoire and has been a featured soloist throughout Europe and the Americas, especially in Chile. However, this trajectory left little scope for a return to Rapa Nui, where piano recitals (and pianos) are scarce. As a solution, Teave turned her focus toward music teaching and raised funds through her worldwide music connections to build a new music school on Rapa Nui, Toki, which she now operates. The fundamental premise for Toki is that music education can provide better social outcomes for young people, and the school operates according to this ethos, providing instruction in classical strings and keyboard side by side with ukulele and other "traditional" performance practices. Teave's success in the classical music context has been followed recently by emerging classical guitarist and composer Moa Edmunds (see Edmunds Guevara 2017).

Another effect was felt on Rapa Nui, where new venues and contexts for music performance emerged, providing opportunities for a wider range of styles. While ostensibly servicing the tourist industry, many of these venues were equally frequented by Rapanui patrons. Perhaps the most radical example of this was Nako—a progressive instrumental rock band with strong heavy metal leanings that had a short but impactful existence in the early 2000s (see Bendrups 2011a). However, other bands with more overt leanings toward traditional, indigenous music also appeared in the pubs and restaurants of Hangaroa at this time, including Varua (meaning ancestor spirit) and Topatangi (an expression indicating nostalgia for a lost loved one).

VARUA

Varua initially came together as the backing band for a recording by Ito Pakarati at the Nuku te Mango studio, but they decided to continue playing together when approached by a local pub that wanted to put on live music for their weekend patrons. The manager of Pub Aloha had a large personal collection of reggae procured from Tahiti (where the popularity of reggae is sufficient to support an annual festival and a constant circulation of French and Caribbean touring acts). This gave Varua a starting point for their own performances, which included various Bob Marley covers (sung in Rapanui language), as well as songs by internationally recognized Chilean reggae band Gondwana (sung in Spanish). Varua was effectively the only "cover band" on Rapa Nui at this time, and their performances were generally well attended.

In a nod to tradition, band leader Julio "Tito" Hotu would commence their performances with a *riu tuai* or, occasionally, an *ute* from his copious personal repertoire, complete with intoned introductions. With a nod to the trans-Pacific flow of cultural influences, their performances always ended with a rendition of Ritchie Valens' *La Bamba*. The band's instrumentation comprised electric guitar, acoustic rhythm guitar, and bass, as well as an improvised drum set assembled by Tito that consisted of two conga drums and a Chilean *bombo*, which he would strike with a mallet while keeping his other hand free to play the congas.

Varua provides a useful example of Rapanui music's twenty-first-century mainstreaming. Tito hails from a family renowned for their musical abilities and possesses a deep knowledge of traditional performance practice, which the band wove into their reggae- and pop-infused original songs. For example, guitarist Terry Crossin's song *Te Moana*, a tribute to the voyage of foundation king Hotu Matu'a, begins with a line from the *riu tuai Ka tomo te Ariki* (one of the songs assembled for the 1938 anniversary celebrations) before the introduction of an electric guitar riff to signal the start of the song proper. In their performances, Varua often extended the *riu tuai* segment of this song, drawing out the phrase and adding *kauaha* and *ngau* on alternating beats. From time to time, members of the audience would join in on the characteristic melismatic phrase endings of the *riu tuai*, which the band would allow to hang in the air before breaking into the electric guitar solo.

TOPATANGI

The band Topatangi emerged from a recording project initiated by Peterico "Pete" Pate in the late 1990s. The band's members had previously been involved with ensembles like Tararaina and with Tapati performances, and Pete was well known for the various *conjunto* songs he had composed on behalf of one Tapati candidate or another over the years. In 1998, Pete's brother died unexpectedly, and after some reflection on his own mortality, he decided that he wanted to preserve his own songs and cultural knowledge on record so that this would be available to his children and grandchildren should he pass away in similar circumstances. However, computers and recording technology were difficult to access on Rapa Nui, and the Nuku te Mango studio had yet to be established, so the opportunity to record was not readily available.

Unbeknownst to Pete, his then-wife Elena, aware of her husband's wishes, began saving and borrowing money to cover the cost of booking a recording studio in Santiago and sending her husband to record there. She called together musicians who had worked with Pete in the past, revealed her plan to Pete, and sent them on a two-week recording trip. This experience galvanized the group, who decided that they would continue performing together on their return to Rapa Nui.

Pete's recording was initially intended mainly for sharing with his own family. However, an airing of their songs on local radio led to Elena being inundated by requests for copies from others, because of the popularity of the songs it contained. As Elena recalled:

> These were Pete's songs, songs which people knew from Tapati over the years, but which were not on any other recordings. Also, the group had a really popular sound. They sounded like a real rock band, like what was popular back when we were younger,

and no other groups on Rapa Nui sounded like that. (Elena Paoa, personal communication, March 10, 2002)

The production of the resulting album, *Moe Varua*, was funded largely through presales. Elena estimated that they sold over three thousand copies on CD and one thousand on cassette, a remarkable result in a community of only around four thousand people. Many of these sales were to the local community, with other copies of *Moe Varua* remaining for the tourist market.

This popularity translated into headline Tapati Rapa Nui performances (well attended by the local community) and a second album for which they received state funding (through FONDART, the Chilean government's primary arts funding council). With other popular performers such as Matato'a and Mito Manutomatoma focused on mainland and international commitments, Topatangi steered their performances toward the local island community.

Topatangi's performance style built on guitar-based *conjunto* repertoire by adding a backline of drum set, electric guitars, and bass. Pete also foregrounded the *upa upa* (an instrument he enjoyed playing) by writing accordion solos into some of his songs. Their catchy rock-inspired tunes (a reminder of the "open house" sessions of the 1960s) were clearly intended for consumption by the Rapanui community. They eschewed the folkloric aesthetics of the island's tourist shows, and they didn't seek to work with dancers or employ typical Rapanui visual elements. Their songs were entirely in Rapanui language, and so were not intended for consumption by mainland Chilean audiences. Instead, Pate composed original songs, drew from *riu* passed down within his family, or occasionally looked to Chile for inspiration, creating Rapanui language covers of rock and pop songs by popular Latin American artists. Their popularity was such that, for a number of years, Pate operated a bar on the Hangaroa main street principally to provide a venue for their weekly performances.

Topatangi was also popular because of the band members' known commitment to community needs. For example, Elena (who was managing the band alongside Pete) steered some of their profits toward charitable needs, such as supporting the local nursing home. Meanwhile, they were also willing supporters of social justice and well-being campaigns. An excellent example of this can be found on their song *Nao nao* (or "mosquito"), composed to assist in a public health campaign (Figure 5.3).

Nao nao was developed in conjunction with the municipal council to draw awareness to an outbreak of dengue fever in 2002. Dengue is not endemic to Rapa Nui but can spread quickly when imported by travelers from elsewhere in the Pacific. The aim of the health campaign was to raise community awareness about the risks posed by dengue fever and to encourage people to remove still water from around their properties to reduce mosquito breeding sites.

The song, which features the energetic ukulele and vocals of Tomas Tepano alongside Pete Pate, is very accessible, built on a very basic I-V-I verse and IV-I-V-I chorus structure, with four-bar phrases. The vocal melody has an accessibly narrow range and is fragmented into bar-length sections, making it easy to remember. Additionally, the verse commences with a chanted

Chanted:

Ina he vai ha'aputu	No stagnant water (means)
Ina he nao nao	No *nao nao*
Ina he nao nao	No *nao nao* (means)
Ina he dengue	No Dengue (fever)

Sung:

Te nao nao e	The *nao nao*
Nao nao tore tore	The one with the little stripes
Patia mai	When he bites
Ahu ahu tatou e	It swells, it swells us all

FIGURE 5.3. *Nao nao* (excerpt).

introduction beseeching the community to eliminate water sources, in order to eliminate mosquitos and thereby eliminate the disease.

CONCLUSION: RAPANUI MUSIC FUTURES

Topatangi's *Nao nao* is a fitting example with which to conclude the discussion of global influences in Rapanui music and to recap the discussion of sustainability in Rapanui music that this book aims to convey. At the height of their popularity, Topatangi were in a privileged social position that would have been recognizable to ancient Rapanui performers, as well as to musicians past and present across the Pacific Islands. Through the power of song, they were being entrusted by cultural authorities to communicate information that was vital to the well-being of the community. To do this, they deployed the most ancient form of Rapanui music making (rhythmic chant) in combination with the most recent form (global pop), producing a song that effectively combined aspects of the present and the past.

By the end of the first decade of the twenty-first century, Topatangi had produced three studio albums, and Matato'a had produced six. Mito Manutomatoma was a household name in Chile, and groups like Kari Kari and Varua had been commissioned to represent Chile in international trade shows and cultural diplomacy missions, just as Tararaina had done in the 1970s. Individual Rapanui musicians were pursuing musical careers as far afield as Hawaii and Australia, while on Rapa Nui, the exponential growth of international tourism provided a seemingly sustainable income source for cultural performance troupes.

Tourist demand for restaurants and bars had created more places for Rapanui musicians to hone their skills. Through Nuku te Mango, at least a dozen local singer-songwriters had recorded albums to sell to tourists at their restaurant gigs. To young performers in particular, music presented an income stream seemingly as viable as any other kind of tourist industry employment in the early twenty-first century.

While the external influence in contemporary Rapanui music is undeniable, contemporary songs are also grounded in an unmistakable sense of belonging to Rapa Nui. The continuity of Rapanui language, and the poetic expression it enables, is at the center of this identity work, but it is also fostered by sonic signifiers—by the particular combination of ukulele and guitar strumming patterns, subtle cross-references to other Rapanui songs, and percussion blueprints that underpin Rapanui musical performances.

Where past generations of Rapanui relied solely on their elders for the transmission of cultural knowledge, a dynamic network of knowledge sources now exists, thanks in part to their engagement with popular music and commercial recording. Ensembles such as Kari Kari offer music and dance apprenticeships in a creative industry context funded privately by tourism. The generation of islanders who experienced the revivalist ethos of Mata Tu'u Hotu Iti have embedded this into their work in contemporary dance studios, music classes, culture workshops, and other pursuits. A heritage repertoire of *riu, riu tuai, ute, patautau,* and *kai kai* has concretized in public knowledge and has a place in contemporary school curricula. Occasionally, musicians will create new songs using the aesthetic features of these ancient performance genres, but for the most part they are content with treating extant traditional repertoire as a bridge to their ancestral past.

Chile remains the primary destination for young Rapanui departing their island for work or study, but where their cultural presence was previously restricted to folklore contexts, they now see their culture reflected in mainstream film, television, and music. The days of waiting for an annual supply ship or traveling to Chile to study for a year at a time are within the living memory of most adult Rapanui, and yet their children operate in global social media circles and negotiate frequent travel back and forth on the now-daily flights between Rapa Nui and Santiago. The world's most remote inhabited island is now no more than a mouse click away.

Rapanui musicians can be found through multiple social media platforms and are primed to engage with new media as it develops. Where videos of Tapati Rapa Nui performances were once virtually unknown, the proliferation of smartphones among Rapa Nui locals and tourists means that a simple internet search will yield hours of footage, presenting the festival from every possible angle, uploaded to video streaming sites. The performance culture that Mito declared to have "arrived" in Chile in 2003 is now omnipresent in the virtual world.

Meanwhile, their grounded places of activity remain strong. Groups such as Kari Kari and Mana Tupuna have built performance venues resembling the *hare koro* of old in which to welcome tourists. Other enterprising islanders offer personalized cultural experiences such as photo shoots and even wedding packages for tourists that draw on the *takona* and *a'amu tuai* practices revived in the 1970s by Mata Tu'u Hotu Iti. None of this would have been possible without the sustained work of musicians over multiple generations to preserve, renew, and replenish their cultural resources. As Jane Moulin (1996) once asserted in her appraisal of Polynesian indigenous music more broadly, considering the cultural loss caused by Western contact in so many instances, "people should stand in awe of its continuity, tenacity, and amazing adaptability instead of shaking their heads over loss or change" (140). The regeneration of Rapanui music, from a population base of barely a hundred people to the rich performance environment of the twenty-first century, must surely be considered among the most remarkable examples of music sustainability.

EPILOGUE

Just as the island has revived from the rubble so many
times in the past . . . why should it not be the case that
the men and women, earth and seed, not also be reborn
every spring and remain beneath their rainbow?

—MARGOT LOYOLA, *contemplating the future*
of Rapanui music (1988: 61)

IN 2003, AFTER VARIOUS MONTHS working together, Papa
Kiko decided to teach me an *ute* that I had not heard before.
He said that he been reflecting on the nature and purpose of
his music and had decided that, as his adoptive son was soon to
be married, a new song was needed to mark the occasion. This
was probably the first *ute* to have been composed since the *ute*
for *ahu* Akivi, which was also one of Papa Kiko's compositions.
Their melodies and structure remained the same, despite the
decades that separated them.

Kiko's son lived on a block of farmland near the center of the
island, obtained through a land restitution project of the Chilean
government. We ordered a taxi to take us there, bouncing over
a dirt road toward a stand of eucalypts imported around thirty
years earlier from Australia. Other guests arrived soon after
by car, on foot, on horseback, and in the Catholic Church's
minibus. Behind these trees, the gateway to the property was
marked with two recently constructed *manavai*—structures
pertaining to precontact Rapa Nui agriculture, consisting of cir-
cular depressions lined with volcanic rock, planted with crops

that benefited from the higher levels of condensation that these depressions collected from the humid air.

Later that evening, at an appropriate hour, Papa Kiko called for the party music to be turned off. Men at Work's "Down Under" gave way to silence, and then the fragile and emotive intonation of *e heraru* emanated from Papa Kiko's throat. As he sang, some of the older folk joined in, first listening to the verse to ensure they understood it and then picking an appropriate part within the *ute* song structure. Soon, the room was reverberating with a tribute to the newly wed couple, sung by an informal ensemble of singers who had not previously heard this song. The sound stopped the children outside from playing with their soccer ball and compelled them to listen. For a moment, there was *mana* in the room. With his song complete, Papa Kiko wiped a tear from his eye and withdrew. The Eagles' "Hotel California" replaced Men at Work on the sound system.

Shortly thereafter, the parish bus returned to pick up the older guests, some young children, Papa Kiko, and myself. The twenty-minute drive back to town was filled with *himene pure*, sung continuously and renewed periodically by different voices drifting in and out. We could still hear the singing from Kiko's porch as the bus pulled away, before it was drowned out by children playing, dogs barking, motorbikes revving, and other Saturday evening sounds.

In his final years, Papa Kiko resolved that his music would not be lost. Where he had previously rebuffed the approaches of some aspiring musicians, he now sought them out to teach them songs that he had guarded closely throughout his lifetime. Where Kiko might once have reserved his energies for a specific protégé, ideally from within his own immediate family, he now invited young people from the many emerging performance troupes to learn from him.

Kiko authorized that the collection of recordings we had made together be shared with the public and charged me with the mission of tracking down and somehow returning to Rapa Nui as many of the other recordings he had made in his lifetime as I could find. These collections now exist for public access in a digital repository within the Rapa Nui museum.

This book conveys a further expression of that impetus to share, to pass on a perspective informed by a lifetime of musical participation grounded in ancient traditions and in Catholic education, encompassing Tahitian influences alongside Chilean ones, and all the while striving to sustain an expressive force that is unique in the world, representing the continuity of Rapanui culture through song. These trans-Pacific cultural forces infused Kiko's musical life, just as they infuse the contemporary reality of Rapanui musicians in the twenty-first century. The faithful repetition of performances preserved by distant ancestors provides a sheltered harbor in which Rapanui musicians can develop and consolidate their musical selves. Meanwhile, the weaving of Polynesian, Latin American, and global influences in Rapanui music provides the raft with which they are able to transcend the boundaries of their remote island home.

GLOSSARY OF RAPANUI MUSICAL

TERMS AND CULTURAL REFERENCES

'Aparima (also kaparima) Line dance, accompanied by upper body
  gestures that reflect aspects of the song text.
'Ei A song of insult or ridicule.
A'amu Story, or legend.
A'amu tuai Ancient story, or legend.
Ahu Ceremonial and burial platform upon which *moai aringa ora*
  were erected.
Ako (te ako) Recitation, or the act of recitation.
Aku aku Ancestor spirit.
'Ao Canoe paddle intended for use as a dance prop (see also *rapa*).
Ariki Chief (or "king").
Ariki mau Paramount chief (or "king").
Ate An ancient song genre.
Ate atua Song of praise (for God).
Ate manava mate Denotes a song of love or nostalgia.
Ate manava more Denotes a more intense song of love or nostalgia.
Bombo Spanish name for a kind of side drum used extensively in
  Chilean folk music.
Conjunto Spanish word for "ensemble," used on Rapa Nui to de-
  scribe guitar-based ensembles that are generally known as "string
  bands" elsewhere in the Pacific.

Haipoipo A wedding, also describes a type of song intended for a wedding.

Haka kakati To improvise, make something up on the spot.

Haka manga To "branch out," used in music to describe compositions inspired or influenced by extant works.

Haka me'eme'e To make fun of someone.

Haka tekateka To gyrate, in dancing.

Haka to'oto'o A guitar technique where the guitar emulates the vocal line.

Hakakio To give thanks, also a song of thanksgiving.

Hami Loin cloth or other apparel made from *mahute*.

Hare koro In precontact Rapanui culture, a structure built to accommodate musical performances.

Hatu The leader of a musical ensemble.

Himene Literally "hymn," derived from Tahitian, but used to describe songs in general on Rapa Nui.

Himene api Literally "new himene," describes newly composed songs.

Himene pure Church hymns and other sacred songs.

Hoko An ancient style of dance, usually accompanied by chanting.

Hui tupana A lineage chant.

Huru riu The Rapanui term for a musical ensemble.

Ihi In ancient music, a high voice.

Kai kai String figures, often with chat accompaniment.

Karanga (krana) A song of welcome.

Kauaha Horse jaw rattle.

Kohau rongorongo "Talking boards"—wooden boards engraved with unique Rapanui script.

Ma'ea haka hetu Large stones traditionally used to accompany singing.

Ma'ea poro Small stones traditionally used to accompany singing.

Mahute Cloth fabricated from beaten paper mulberry stems.

Manu (Manu tupana) An obsolete performance genre, possibly for lineage chants.

Miro o'one "Earth boat," a feature of early twentieth-century Rapanui celebrations.

Moai (moai aringa ora) Statues characteristic of Rapa Nui, carved to resemble human forms and placed upon *ahu* in precontact times.

Moko Lizard.

Motuha Traditionally an organizer or patron of a celebration.

Neru In precontact times, children who were specially selected to be secluded and trained for ceremonial purposes.

Ngau Literally "throat," describes grunts and other nonverbal noises produced from the performer's throat while singing.

Nua "Mother," also "grandmother."

Paina Festival, and effigy used in a festival.

Paina tuhi renga Festival of presentation.

Pascuense Literally "Pascuan" (pertaining to Isla de Pascua).

Patautau Traditional rhythmic chant.

Peho A slang Rapanui tem for "song."

Pepere In ancient music, a low/male voice.

Pu Wind, also "blow."

Pukeho A unique precontact percussion instrument formed from a slate sounding board in a chest-depth hole.

Punipuni Early twentieth-century record player.

Rapa A kind of dancing paddle (see also *Ao*).

Reina de la primavera The "Spring Queen" annual cultural festival and competition in Chile.

Re'o araro Soprano voice.

Re'o arunga Alto voice.

Re'o vaenga Tenor voice.

Re'o vaenga araro Bass voice.

Riu The traditional Rapanui term for "song."

Riu tangi Laments, also songs expressing other kinds of strong emotion.

Riu tuai Ancient or "old" songs.

Sau sau A popular song that emerged in the 1940s and that is considered iconic of Rapa Nui, especially in mainland Chile.

Ta hatirati A dance stemming from the early twentieth century in which the dancers imitate Western sailors.

Takona Traditional body painting.

Tangata manu Literally "bird man," the basis of an important precontact ritual.

Tango Rapanui The unique Rapa Nui variant of tango.

Tapu Something that is sacred, or prohibited.

Te ori Dance.

Tekateka A signaling device believed to have been used in traditional performances.

Tumu ivi atua A "witch" or shaman.

Ua A ceremonial staff used in performances.

Upa upa Accordion.

Ute A traditional song genre believed to have been introduced from Tahiti in the late nineteenth century.

Va'e Literally "foot" or "lower leg," denotes the person playing the *pukeho* in ancient Rapanui performances.

REFERENCES

Abarca, Sofía. 2015. *Ríu, el canto primal de Rapa Nui*. Santiago: LOM Ediciones.

Alexeyeff, Kalissa. 2003. "Dancing from the Heart: Movement, Gender and Sociality in the Cook Islands." PhD diss., Australian National University, Canberra.

Arredondo, Anna Maria. 2004. *Takona Tatu*. Hangaroa: Rapanui Press.

Auclair, Elizabeth, and Graeme Fairclough, eds. 2015. *Theory and Practice in Heritage and Sustainability: Between Past and Future*. Abingdon: Routledge.

Ayres, William S., and Gabriela S. Ayres. 1995. *Geiseler's Easter Island Report: An 1880s Anthropological Account*. Honolulu: Social Science Research Institute, University of Hawaii.

Barthel, Thomas S. 1978. *The Eighth Land: The Polynesian Discovery and Settlement of Easter Island*. Honolulu: University of Hawaii Press.

Beaglehole, J. C., ed. 1969. *The Journals of Captain Cook*, Vol. 2: *The Voyage of the Resolution and Adventure 1772–1775*. Cambridge: Cambridge University Press.

Beechey, F. W. 1831. *Narrative of a Voyage to the Pacific and Beering's Strait (1825 to 1828)*. Vol. 1. London: Henry Colburn and Richard Bentley.

Bello, Joakin. 1995. *Chants from Rapa Nui*. Total Music, CTM211011, compact disc.

Bendrups, Dan. 2006a. "Continuity in Adaptation: A History of Rapanui Music." PhD diss., Macquarie University, Sydney.

Bendrups, Dan. 2006b. "War in Rapanui Music: A History of Cultural Representation." *Yearbook for Traditional Music* 38: 18–32.

Bendrups, Dan. 2007a. "Easter Island Music and the Voice of Kiko Pate: A Biographical History of Sound Recording." *World of Music* 49 (1): 112–27.

Bendrups, Dan. 2007b. "Oceanic Encounters on Record: The Social History and Significance of the Rapanui Song Sausau." In *Oceanic Music Encounters: Essays in Honour of Mervyn McLean*, edited by Richard Moyle, 35–45. Auckland: RAL.

Bendrups, Dan. 2009a. "*Navegando, Navegando*: Easter Island Fusion and Cultural Performance." *Asia Pacific Journal of Anthropology* 10 (2): 115–28.

Bendrups, Dan. 2009b. "Sounds of Easter Island: Music and Cultural Representation in *Ogú y Mampato en Rapanui*." *Animation Journal* 17: 72–85.

Bendrups, Dan. 2010. "Fusión Rapa Nui: Mito Manutomatoma and the Translocation of Easter Island Music in Chilean Popular Culture." In *Cultural Transformations: Perspectives on Translocation in a Global Age*, edited by Chris Prentice, Vijay Devidas, and Henry Johnson, 137–58. Amsterdam: Rodopi.

Bendrups, Dan. 2011a. "Nako: The Metal in the Marrow of Easter Island Music." In *Metal Rules the Globe: Heavy Metal Music around the World*, edited by Jeremy Wallach, Harris M. Berger, and Paul D. Greene, 313–32. Durham, NC: Duke University Press.

Bendrups, Dan. 2011b. "Latin Down Under: Latin American Migrant Musicians in Australia and New Zealand." *Popular Music* 30 (2): 191–207.

Bendrups, Dan. 2011c. "Performing Austronesia in the Twenty-First Century: A Rapa Nui Perspective on Shared Culture and Contact." In *Austronesian Soundscapes: Performing Arts in Oceania and Southeast Asia*, edited by Birgit Abels, 261–76. Amsterdam: Amsterdam University Press.

Bendrups, Dan. 2013. "Popular Music, Cultural Policy, and the Festival of Pacific Arts." *Perfect Beat* 14 (2): 157–73.

Bendrups, Dan. 2016a. "Performing Trans-Pacific Identities: The Role of Music and Musicians in Interactions between Easter Island and

Chile." In *Transpacific Americas: Encounters and Engagements between the Americas and the South Pacific*, edited by Eveline Durr and Philipp Schorch, 27–41. London: Routledge.

Bendrups, Dan. 2016b. "A Folk Song Prodigy? Considering the Exceptional Musical Childhood of Chilean Folklorist Margot Loyola." In *Child Prodigies in Music*, edited by Gary McPherson, 638–47. New York: Oxford.

Bendrups, Dan, Kate Barney, and Catherine Grant. 2013. "An Introduction to Sustainability and Ethnomusicology in the Australasian Context." *Musicology Australia* 35 (2): 153–58.

Bendrups, Dan, Pip Laufiso, and Hiliako Iaheto. 2018. "'Koile, 'Te Hua' and the Reggae-fication of Cultural Heritage." In *The Routledge Companion to Popular Music History and Heritage*, edited by Sarah Baker, Catherine Strong, Lauren Istvandity, and Zelmarie Cantillon, 326–35. Abingdon: Routledge.

Blixen, Olaf. 1979. "Figuras de Hilo Tradicionales de la Isla de Pascua y sus correspondientes salmodias." *Moana* 2 (1): 1–106.

Bork, Hans-Rudolf, and Andreas Mieth. 2003. "The Key Role of Jubea Palm Trees in the History of Rap Nui: A Provocative Interpretation." *Rapa Nui Journal* 17 (2): 119–21.

Campbell, Ramón. 1971. *La herencia musical de Rapanui: Etnomusicología de la Isla de Pascua*. Santiago: Editorial Andres Bello.

Campbell, Ramón. 1988. "Etnomusicología de la Isla de Pascua." *Revista Musical Chilena* 42 (170): 5–47.

Castro Flores, Nelson. 2006. *El Diablo, Dios y la Profetisa*. Hangaroa: Rapanui Press.

Comisión verdad historica y nuevo trato de Isla de Pascua. 2001. *La verdad histórica de Rapa Nui*. Ministerio del Interior y Provincia de Valparaíso, decreto supremo 19.

Conrich, Ian, and Hermann Mückler, eds. 2016. *Rapa Nui - Easter Island: Cultural and Historical Perspectives*. Berlin: Frank & Timme.

Dannemann, Manuel. 2007. *Cultura Folclórica de Chile*. Santiago: Editorial Universitaria.

Dening, Greg. 1996. *Performances*. Melbourne: The University of Melbourne Press.

Diamond, Jared. 2005. *Collapse: How Societies Choose to Fail or Succeed*. New York: Viking Press.

Edmunds Guevara, Moa. 2017. *Confluencia*. Valparaíso: Cadenza Editorial.

Englert, Sebastian. 1964. *Primer siglo cristiano de la Isla de Pascua*. Frankfurt: Vurvuert.

Englert, Sebastian. 1970. *Island at the Center of the World: New Light on Easter Island*. Translated by William Mulloy. London: Robert Hale and Company.

Englert, Sebastian. 1995. *La tierra de Hotu Matu'a: Historia y etnologia de la Isla de Pascua*. 7th ed. Santiago: Editorial Universitaria.

Englert, Sebastian. 2002. *Legends of Easter Island*. Rapa Nui: Father Sebastian Englert Anthropological Museum.

Estella, Bienvenido. 1920. *Los misterios de la Isla Pascua*. Santiago: Imprenta Cervantes.

Fehren-Schmitz, Lars, Caterine L. Jarman, Keely M. Harkins, Manfred Kayser, Brian N. Popp, and Pontus Skoglund. 2014. "Genetic Ancestry of Rapanui before and after European Contact." *Current Biology* 27 (20): 3209–15.

Felbermayer, Francisco. 1972. "Leider und Verse der Oster-Insel." *Zeitschrift für Ethnologie* 97 (2): 268–82.

Fischer, Hermann. 2001. *Sombras sobre Rapa Nui: Alegato por un pueblo olvidado*. 2nd ed. Santiago: LOM Ediciones.

Fischer, Stephen. 2005. *Island at the End of the World: The Turbulent History of Easter Island*. London: Reaktion.

Flannery, Timothy. 1994. *The Future Eaters*. Sydney: Reed Books.

Flenley, John, and Paul Bahn. 2003. *The Enigmas of Easter Island*. 2nd ed. London: Oxford University Press.

Fortin, Moira. 2009. "The Development of Theatre in Easter Island - Hakararama i te A'amu o Rapa Nui." Master's diss., University of Otago, Dunedin.

Garrido, Waldo, and Dan Bendrups. 2013. "Transcultural Latino: Negotiating Music Industry Expectations of Latin American Migrant Musicians in Australasia." *Musicology Australia* 35 (1): 1–15.

González, Juan Pablo, and Claudio Rolle. 2005. *Historia Social de la Música Popular en Chile 1890–1950*. Santiago: Ediciones Universidad Católica de Chile.

Grant, Catherine. 2014. *Music Endangerment: How Language Maintenance Can Help*. New York: Oxford University Press.

Grant, Catherine, and Huib Schippers, eds. 2016. *Sustainable Futures for Music Cultures: An Ecological Perspective.* New York: Oxford University Press.

Hacker, Carlotta. 1968. . . . *And Christmas Day on Easter Island.* London: Michael Joseph.

Heyerdahl, Thor. 1972. *Aku-Aku: The Secret of Easter Island.* 7th ed. London: Penguin.

Hotus, Alberto, and Comisión Para la Estructuración de la Lengua Rapanui. 2000. *Diccionario Etimológico Rapanui-Español.* Valparaíso: Universidad de Playa Ancha.

Hotus, Alberto, and Consejo de Jefes Rapanui. 1988. *Te Mau Hatu'O Rapa Nui.* Santiago: Editorial Emisión and Centro de Estudio Latinoamericano Simón Bolivar.

Huke, Paloma. 1995. *Mata Tu'u Hotu Iti: Revelando Misterios.* Santiago: Tiempo Nuevo.

Hunt, Terry L., and Carl P. Lipo. 2006. "Late Colonization of Easter Island." *Science* 311 (5767): 1603–606.

Jolly, Margaret. 1992. "Spectres of Inauthenticity." *Contemporary Pacific* 4 (1): 49–72.

Jolly, Margaret, and Nick Thomas. 1992. "Introduction." *Oceania, Special Issue: The Politics of Tradition in the Pacific* 62 (4): 241–48.

Kaeppler, Adrienne. 1980. "Polynesian Music and Dance." In *Music of Many Cultures,* edited by Elizabeth May, 134–53. Los Angeles: University of California Press.

Kaeppler, Adrienne. 2001. "Accordions in Tahiti: An Enigma." In *Traditionalism and Modernity in the Music and Dance of Oceania: Essays in Honour of Barbara B. Smith,* edited by Helen R. Lawrence and Don Niles, 45–66. Sydney: University of Sydney.

Kaeppler, Adrienne, and Juan Pablo González. 1998. "Rapanui." In *The Garland Encyclopedia of World Music,* Vol. 9: *Australia and the Pacific Islands,* edited by Adrienne Kaeppler and Jacob Love, 951–53. New York: Garland Publishing.

Kieviet, Paulus. 2016. "A Grammar of Rapa Nui: The Language of Easter Island." PhD diss., Vrije Universiteit, Amsterdam.

Larsen, Annegret, and Dale F. Simpson Jr. 2014. "Comment to Rull et al. (2013)—Challenging Easter Island's Collapse: The Need for Interdisciplinary Synergies." *Frontiers in Ecology and Evolution* 15. doi:https://doi.org/10.3389/fevo.2014.00056.

Linkels, Ad. 2000. "Polynesia: The Real Music of Paradise." In *World Music: The Rough Guide*, edited by Simon Broughton and Mark Ellingham, 218–29. London: Rough Guides.

Linkels, Ad, and Lucia Linkels. 1999. *Hula, Haka, Hoko! An Introduction to Polynesian Dancing*. Tilburg: Mundo Étnico Foundation.

Loti, Pierre. 1899. *Reflets sur la sombre route*. Paris: Calmann-Lévy.

Loti, Pierre. 1988 [1899]. *L'Ile de Pâques: Journal d'un aspirant de La Flore*. Ville-d'Avray: Éditions Pierre-Olivier Combelles.

Loyola, Margot. 1988. "Mis vivencias in Isla de Pascua." *Revista Musical Chilena* 42 (170): 48–86.

Macmillan-Brown, John. 1926. *The Riddle of the Pacific*. 3rd ed. London: Fisher Unwin.

Manutomatoma, Mito. 2003. *Mito y Fusión Rapa Nui*. Warner Music Chile, 092749869-2, compact disc.

Matato'a. 1998. *Tama'i*. Matato'a Production, compact disc.

Matato'a. 2004. *Tamai*. https://www.youtube.com/watch?v=iXY_Drfz_PU.

Maude, Henry E. 1981. *Slavers in Paradise: The Peruvian Slave Trade in Polynesia, 1862–1864*. Stanford, CA: Stanford University Press.

McCall, Grant. 1975. "Sympathy and Antipathy in Easter Islander and Chilean Relations." *Journal of the Polynesian Society* 84 (4): 467–76.

McCall, Grant. 1994. *Rapanui: Tradition and Survival on Easter Island*. 2nd ed. Sydney: Allen and Unwin.

McCall, Grant, and Dan Bendrups. 2008. "Luis (Avaka) Pate Paoa: A Tribute." *The Journal of the Polynesian Society* 117 (4): 405–407.

McLean, Mervyn. 1999. *Weavers of Song: Polynesian Music and Dance*. Auckland: Auckland University Press.

Mètraux, Alfred. 1940. *Ethnology of Easter Island*. Honolulu: Bishop Museum Press.

Mètraux, Alfred. 1957. *Easter Island: A Stone Age Civilization of the Pacific*. London: Andrew Deutsch.

Moulin, Jane. 1996. "What's Mine Is Yours? Cultural Borrowing in a Pacific Context." *Contemporary Pacific* 8 (1): 128–53.

Moyle, Richard. 1990. *Polynesian Sound-Producing Instruments*. Princes Risborough: Shire Publications.

Moyle, Richard. 1991. *Polynesian Music and Dance*. Auckland: Centre for Pacific Studies.

Novitski, Joseph. 1970. "Closing of U.S. Base Stirs Easter Island." *New York Times*, November 9, p. 3.

Pakarati, I., M. Rauch, and P. Avila. 1995. *Kai Kai: sentimento y cuerpo de la tradición oral Rapa Nui*. Santiago: Independent production.

Pakomio, Jorge. 2004. *Hakaora Koe—Rapa Nui In*. Santiago, Raf Sound System, compact disc.

Palazzo, Anna Laura, and Antonio Pugliano. 2015. "The Burden of History: Living Heritage and Everyday Life in Rome." In *Theory and Practice in Heritage and Sustainability: Between Past and Future*, edited by Elizabeth Auclair and Graeme Fairclough, 54–68. Abingdon: Routledge.

Peiser, Benny. 2005. "From Genocide to Ecocide: The Rape of Rapa Nui." *Energy and Environment* 16: 513–40.

Pereira-Salas, Eugenio. 1947. "La musica de la Isla de Pascua." *Revista Musical Chilena* 45 (176): 142.

Pettan, Svanibor, and Jeff T. Titon, eds. 2015. *The Oxford Handbook for Applied Ethnomusicology*. New York: Oxford University Press.

Pignet, L. 2001. *"Kai Kai*: Tradition and Innovation on Rapa Nui." In *Pacific 2000: Proceedings of the Fifth International Conference on Easter Island and the Pacific*, edited by Christopher Stevenson, Georgia Lee, and F. Morin, 373–76. Los Osos: Easter Island Foundation, in conjunction with Bearsville Press.

Ponting, Clive. 1991. *A Green History of the World: The Environment and the Collapse of Great Civilizations*. New York: Penguin.

Porteous, John Douglas. 1981. *The Modernization of Easter Island*. Western Geographical Series 19. Victoria: University of Victoria (B.C.).

Reynolds, Kevin, dir. 1994. *Rapa Nui*. Warner Bros 6303333141, USA.

Routledge, Katherine. 1998 [1919]. *The Mystery of Easter Island*. Kempton: Adventures Unlimited Press.

Santa Coloma, Maria Elena. 2006. *Rapa Nui: Guardianes de la tradición*. Hangaroa: Rapanui Press.

Schippers, Huib, and Dan Bendrups. 2015. "Ethnomusicology, Ecology and Sustainable Music Cultures." *World of Music* 4 (1): 9–19.

Sierra, Malu. 2002. *Rapanui: náufragos del planeta*. Santiago: Editorial Persona.

Stanton, Max. 2003. "Economics and Tourism Development on Easter Island." In *Pacific Island Tourism*, edited by David Harrison, 110–24. New York: Cognizant Communication Corporation.

Stevenson, Christopher M., Cedric O. Puleston, Peter M. Vitousek, Oliver A. Chadwick, Sonia Haoa, and Thegn N. Ladefoged. 2015. "Variation in Rapa Nui (Easter Island) Land Use Indicates Production and Population Peaks Prior to European Contact." *PNAS* 112 (4): 1025–30.

Teao, Kio. 1983. *Ka Hoko Mai.* Pamigraf Chile, cassette.

Thomas, Allan. 1981. "The Study of Acculturated Music in Oceania: 'Cheap and Tawdry Borrowed Tunes'?" *Journal of the Polynesian Society* 90 (2): 183–92.

Thompson, William J. 1891. "Te Pito te Henua or Easter Island." In *Annual Report of the Board of Regents of the Smithsonian Institution.* Washington, DC: Smithsonian Institution.

Tuki, P., A. Mahina, and C. Paoa. 1991. *Actividades fisico-deportivas y y culturales realizadas en la fiesta de la Tapati Rapa-Nui.* Undergraduate thesis, Universidad Católica de Valparaiso, Valparaíso.

Unattributed. 1895. *Boletin de las Leyes i Decretos del Gobierno volumen 1, libro LXIV.* Santiago: Gobierno de Chile.

Unattributed. 1944. "Nativos de la Isla de Pascua siguen de actualidad: cantaron por Radio." *La Nación,* in the William Mulloy Library Newspaper Archive 67 (23). Hangaroa: Wiliam Mulloy Library.

UNESCO. 2003. *Declaration on Intangible Cultural Heritage.* https://ich.unesco.org/.

UNESCO. 2005. *Convention on the Protection and Promotion of the Diversity of Cultural Expressions.* www.unesco.org/culture/dce.

UNESCO. 2012. *Reconocimiento de excellencia de al UNESCO para los productos artesanales del MERCOSUR+ (Argentina, Brasil, Chile, Paraguay y Uruguay).* Montevideo: Oficina Regional de Ciencia para America Latina y el Caribe.

United Nations. 2007. *Declaration on the Rights of Indigenous Peoples.* https://www.un.org/development/desa/indigenouspeoples/declaration-on-the-rights-of-indigenous-peoples.html.

Urrutia Blondel, Jorge. 1958. "Reportaje de un musico a Rapa-Nui." *Revista Musical Chilena* 12 (60): 5–47.

van Tilberg, Jo-Anne. 1994. *Easter Island: Archaeology, Ecology and Culture.* London: British Museum Press.

Vargas Santander, Patricia. 1988. "Los grillos de Pascua." *Revista de Educacion* 159: 39–44.

von Däniken, Erich. 1968. *Memories of the Future: Unresolved Mysteries of the Past.* New York: Putnam.

Wilhelm, O. 1935. "Historia de Isla de Pascua." *Revista de Marina* 464: 1–21.

Zamora, R., A. Lucas, J. Lucas, and T. Rapu. 1995. *Propuesta pedagogica para le enseñanza de la cultura pascuence en los cursos de septimo y octavo año basico de Rapa Nui.* Undergraduate diss., Pontifica Universidad Católica de Chile, Santiago.

INDEX